Ultimate Salad Cookbook

Over 100 Easy and Delicious Recipes for Every Occasion – Master the Basics with Everyday Ingredients | Full Color Edition

Emily Mia Barrett

Copyright

This book is copyright © 2025 by Emily Mia Barrett. All rights are reserved. Any unauthorized reproduction, sharing, or distribution of this work, in part or in its entirety, is strictly prohibited. This includes any form of digital or analog replica, such as photocopying, recording, or information storage and retrieval systems, except as permitted under sections of copyright law for brief quotations in a review.

Legal Disclaimer

The material presented in this book is intended for informational purposes only. No warranty, express or implied, on the quality, precision, or suitability for a particular purpose of the content is offered. The author shall not be held responsible for any direct, consequential, or incidental damages arising from using or misusing any information herein. While every effort has been made to ensure the accuracy of the material in this book, neither the author nor the publisher accepts responsibility for any mistakes, inaccuracies, or omissions. If you need professional advice, please consult a qualified professional.

Your purchase and use of this book indicate your acceptance of these terms and conditions.

Table of Content

Ultimate Salad Cookbook 1
Introduction 5
Understanding Salad Ingredients 6
Tools and Tips for Salad Making 9
Classic Green Salads 12
    Simple Caesar Salad 13
    Mixed Greens With Lemon Vinaigrette 13
    Spinach And Strawberry Salad 14
    Arugula And Parmesan Salad 14
    Garden Salad With Ranch Dressing 15
    Kale And Apple Salad 15
    Butter Lettuce With Herbs 16
    Classic Cobb Salad 16
    Baby Greens With Balsamic Vinaigrette 17
    Romaine And Radish Salad 17
    Green Bean And Almond Salad 18
    Watercress And Avocado Salad 18
    Endive And Orange Salad 19
    Bibb Lettuce With Dijon Dressing 19
    Cucumber And Mint Salad 20
    Beet And Goat Cheese Salad 20
Crunchy Veggie Salads 21
    Carrot And Raisin Salad 22
    Classic Coleslaw 22
    Asian Slaw With Peanut Dressing 23
    Cucumber And Tomato Salad 23
    Broccoli And Cheddar Salad 24
    Jicama And Citrus Salad 24
    Crunchy Radish Salad 25
    Bell Pepper And Corn Salad 25
    Zucchini Ribbon Salad 26
    Rainbow Slaw With Lime Dressing 26
    Marinated Mushroom Salad 27
    Cabbage And Apple Slaw 27
    Snap Pea And Radish Salad 28
    Spicy Kimchi Slaw 28
    Carrot And Beet Salad 29
    Fennel And Orange Salad 29
Hearty Grain and Bean Salads 30
    Quinoa And Black Bean Salad 31
    Mediterranean Farro Salad 31
    Barley And Roasted Vegetable Salad 32
    Wild Rice And Cranberry Salad 32
    Chickpea And Cucumber Salad 33
    Bulgur And Parsley Salad 33
    Lentil And Feta Salad 34
    Couscous And Tomato Salad 34
    Brown Rice And Avocado Salad 35
    Orzo And Spinach Salad 35
    Three-Bean Salad 36
    Freekeh And Kale Salad 36
    Wheatberry And Pomegranate Salad 37
    Black-Eyed Pea Salad 37
    Spelt And Roasted Pepper Salad 38
    Tabbouleh Salad 38
Protein-Packed Tofu and Egg Salads 39
    Tofu Caesar Salad 40
    Curried Tofu Salad 40
    Tofu And Mango Salad 41
    Grilled Tofu And Vegetable Salad 41
    Tofu And Avocado Salad 42
    Spicy Tofu And Noodle Salad 42
    Tofu And Spinach Salad 43
    Tofu And Edamame Salad 43
    Classic Egg Salad 44
    Deviled Egg Salad 44
    Egg And Bacon Salad 45
    Egg And Potato Salad 45
    Egg And Avocado Salad 46
    Egg And Tomato Salad 46
    Egg And Cucumber Salad 47
    Mediterranean Egg Salad 47

Light and Fresh Seafood Salads 48
    Classic Tuna Salad 49
    Shrimp And Avocado Salad 49
    Crab And Corn Salad 50
    Salmon And Dill Salad 50
    Smoked Salmon And Cucumber Salad 51
    Scallop And Mango Salad 51
    Seafood Pasta Salad 52
    Lobster And Asparagus Salad 52
    Calamari And Tomato Salad 53
    Prawn And Watermelon Salad 53
    Sardine And Potato Salad 54
    Octopus And Olive Salad 54
    Mackerel And Beet Salad 55
    Tuna Niçoise Salad 55
    Grilled Shrimp Caesar Salad 56
    Spicy Crab Salad 56

Flavorful Chicken Salads 57
    Classic Chicken Caesar Salad 58
    Bbq Chicken Salad 58
    Asian Chicken Salad 59
    Chicken And Avocado Salad 59
    Grilled Chicken And Quinoa Salad 60
    Chicken And Mango Salad 60
    Chicken And Bacon Ranch Salad 61
    Chicken And Spinach Salad 61
    Mediterranean Chicken Salad 62
    Chicken And Apple Salad 62
    Chicken And Pineapple Salad 63
    Chicken And Chickpea Salad 63
    Buffalo Chicken Salad 64
    Chicken And Orzo Salad 64
    Chicken And Kale Salad 65
    Honey Mustard Chicken Salad 65

Savory Meat Salads 66
    Classic Beef Salad 67
    Steak And Blue Cheese Salad 67
    Pork And Apple Salad 68
    Lamb And Mint Salad 68
    Roast Beef And Arugula Salad 69

    Ham And Cheddar Salad 69
    Turkey And Cranberry Salad 70
    Bacon And Egg Salad 70
    Prosciutto And Melon Salad 71
    Chorizo And Potato Salad 71
    Duck And Orange Salad 72
    Venison And Beet Salad 72
    Sausage And Lentil Salad 73
    Chicken Liver And Onion Salad 73
    Corned Beef And Cabbage Salad 74
    Meatball And Pasta Salad 74

Conclusion 75
Index 76

Introduction

Welcome to the **Ultimate Salad Cookbook**, where you'll discover the joy of creating fresh, delicious, and nutritious salads with ease. This book is designed to be your go-to guide for everything salad, whether you're a seasoned cook or just starting your culinary journey. Our goal is to simplify the art of salad-making, making it accessible and enjoyable for everyone.

Salads are more than just a side dish; they can be a vibrant and satisfying main course, a refreshing snack, or a perfect complement to any meal. With the right combination of ingredients, a salad can be a delightful explosion of flavors, colors, and textures. This book offers over 100 easy-to-follow recipes that use everyday ingredients to create a wide range of salads, from classic green salads to hearty grain and protein-packed options.

Before we dive into the recipes, we'll take a moment to explore the fundamentals of salad-making. Understanding the ingredients and having the right tools are key to creating the perfect salad. In the following chapters, you'll find a detailed guide on the essential ingredients and tips for choosing the freshest produce, along with a rundown of the tools that will make your salad preparation effortless.

Whether you're looking to create a simple salad for a quick meal or something more elaborate to impress your guests, this book has you covered. Get ready to master the art of salad-making and enjoy the endless possibilities that salads have to offer.

Understanding Salad Ingredients

To create a truly delicious and memorable salad, it's important to start with a solid understanding of the ingredients you'll be using. This chapter will guide you through the essentials of salad ingredients, helping you make the best choices to elevate your salads to the next level.

Greens

The foundation of most salads, greens come in a variety of textures, flavors, and nutritional profiles. From the crisp bite of romaine to the peppery kick of arugula, each type of green adds a unique element to your salad. Here's a quick overview of some popular greens:

- **Romaine Lettuce:** Crisp and sturdy, great for Caesar salads.
- **Spinach:** Tender and mild, packed with vitamins and minerals.
- **Arugula:** Peppery and bold, perfect for adding a bit of spice.
- **Kale:** Hearty and slightly bitter, excellent for nutrient-dense salads.
- **Mixed Greens:** A blend of various greens, offering a mix of textures and flavors.

Vegetables

Vegetables add color, crunch, and nutrition to your salads. The key is to use a variety of vegetables to keep your salads interesting and flavorful. Some popular choices include:

- **Tomatoes:** Juicy and sweet, a classic addition to any salad.
- **Cucumbers:** Crisp and refreshing, they add a cooling element.
- **Bell Peppers:** Vibrant and crunchy, available in a range of colors.
- **Carrots:** Sweet and crunchy, they add a nice texture contrast.
- **Avocado:** Creamy and rich, providing healthy fats and a satisfying mouthfeel.

Fruits

Adding fruit to your salad can bring a surprising burst of sweetness and freshness. Fruits pair wonderfully with greens and vegetables, balancing flavors and adding a unique twist. Consider using:

- **Berries (strawberries, blueberries, raspberries):** Sweet and tart, they add a pop of color and flavor.
- **Citrus (oranges, grapefruit):** Juicy and tangy, perfect for a refreshing contrast.

- **Apples and Pears:** Crisp and slightly sweet, they add a satisfying crunch.
- **Dried Fruits (raisins, cranberries):** Chewy and sweet, they bring a different texture to your salad.

Proteins

Adding protein turns your salad into a complete meal. Whether you're looking for plant-based options or more traditional proteins, there are plenty of choices:

- **Grilled Chicken:** A lean, versatile protein that pairs well with most salads.
- **Tofu:** A plant-based option that absorbs flavors and adds a firm texture.
- **Hard-Boiled Eggs:** Rich and satisfying, they add a creamy texture.
- **Legumes (chickpeas, black beans):** High in protein and fiber, perfect for heartier salads.
- **Seafood (shrimp, tuna, salmon):** Light and flavorful, adding a taste of the sea to your salad.

Grains and Nuts

For added texture and substance, grains and nuts are excellent choices. They can transform a light salad into a more filling dish:

- **Quinoa:** A protein-packed grain with a slightly nutty flavor.
- **Farro:** Chewy and hearty, great for adding bulk to your salad.
- **Almonds, Walnuts, Pecans:** Crunchy and rich in healthy fats, they add a delightful texture contrast.

- **Seeds (pumpkin, sunflower, chia):** Tiny but mighty, they add crunch and a boost of nutrition.

Cheeses

Cheese can add creaminess, saltiness, and richness to your salads. Whether you prefer a crumbly blue cheese or a soft mozzarella, cheese can enhance the flavor profile of your salad:

- **Feta:** Tangy and crumbly, a staple in Mediterranean salads.
- **Parmesan:** Sharp and salty, perfect for shaving over greens.
- **Goat Cheese:** Creamy and slightly tangy, pairs well with fruits.
- **Cheddar:** Bold and flavorful, adds a sharp contrast to sweeter ingredients.

Dressings

A salad is never complete without a dressing to tie all the ingredients together. Whether you prefer a light vinaigrette or a creamy dressing, the choice of dressing can make or break your salad. Some popular types include:

- **Vinaigrettes (balsamic, lemon, red wine):** Light and tangy, they enhance the natural flavors of the ingredients.
- **Creamy Dressings (Caesar, ranch, blue cheese):** Rich and indulgent, they add a luxurious texture.
- **Citrus-Based Dressings:** Refreshing and zesty, perfect for cutting through rich ingredients.

By understanding the role each ingredient plays, you can begin to experiment and create your own perfect salads. The key is to balance flavors, textures, and colors to make a salad that is not only nutritious but also a delight to eat. As you explore the recipes in this book, keep these fundamentals in mind to maximize your salad-making potential.

Tools and Tips for Salad Making

Creating the ideal salad is more than simply choosing the correct ingredients; having the appropriate equipment and following some basic guidelines may make the process easier, more efficient, and more pleasurable. In this chapter, we'll go over the necessary equipment you'll need as well as some helpful techniques for keeping your salads fresh, tasty, and elegantly presented.

Essential Tools for Salad Making

Salad Spinner

A salad spinner is an indispensable tool for drying greens. It ensures that your lettuce and other leafy greens are crisp and free from excess water, which can dilute dressings and make salads soggy.

Sharp Chef's Knife

A high-quality chef's knife is essential for accurately cutting, slicing, and dicing food. A sharp knife not only simplifies the process, but it also helps to preserve the freshness of delicate components such as tomatoes and herbs.

Cutting Board

Invest in a sturdy, non-slip cutting board. It provides a stable surface for preparing ingredients and can help prevent cross-contamination when working with different food types.

Mixing Bowls

A collection of mixing bowls of different sizes is required for tossing salads, making dressings, and marinating components. Bowls made of stainless steel or glass are long-lasting and simple to clean.

Tongs

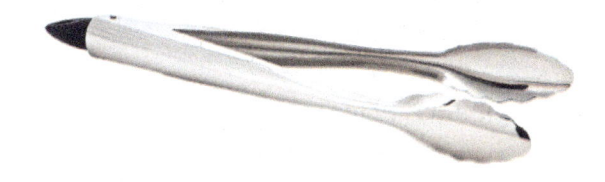

Tongs are perfect for tossing and serving salads without bruising delicate greens. They give you better control and help evenly distribute dressings.

Measuring Cups and Spoons

Accurate measurements are key, especially when making dressings or following recipes. A good set of measuring cups and spoons ensures consistency in your salad-making.

Vegetable Peeler

A vegetable peeler is useful for creating thin ribbons of vegetables like carrots or zucchini, adding texture and visual appeal to your salads.

Mandoline Slicer

For precise, uniform slices of vegetables and fruits, a mandoline slicer is a fantastic tool. It's great for quickly preparing ingredients like cucumbers, radishes, or beets.

Grater or Microplane

A grater or microplane is handy for adding finely grated cheese, zesting citrus fruits, or grating garlic directly into dressings.

Salad Servers

Dedicated salad servers make it easy to toss and serve salads without damaging delicate ingredients. They also add a touch of elegance when serving guests.

Tips for Making the Perfect Salad

Start with Fresh Ingredients

Fresh, high-quality ingredients are the cornerstone of a delicious salad. Choose sharp greens, ripe veggies, and fresh herbs for the best taste and nutrients.

Dry Your Greens Thoroughly

After washing your greens, use a salad spinner to remove excess water. This helps the dressing adhere better and prevents your salad from becoming watery.

Cut Ingredients Uniformly

Try to cut your salad ingredients into uniform pieces. This not only makes your salad look more appealing but also ensures even distribution of flavors in every bite.

Season Your Greens

Before adding dressing, lightly season your greens with a pinch of salt. This enhances the natural flavors and makes the salad more flavorful.

Balance Textures

A great salad has a mix of textures—crunchy, soft, chewy, and creamy. Consider adding nuts, seeds, croutons, or soft cheeses to create contrast and interest.

Dressings: Less is More

Start with a small amount of dressing and add more if needed. Overdressing can make a salad soggy, while underdressing can leave it dry. Aim for just enough to coat the ingredients lightly.

Toss Gently

Use tongs or your hands to toss the salad gently. This ensures that all the ingredients are evenly coated without bruising the greens.

Add Delicate Ingredients Last

Save delicate ingredients like avocado, berries, or crumbled cheese for last. Add them just before serving to keep them intact and looking fresh.

Experiment with Flavors

Don't be hesitant to try new taste combinations. To improve your salad, add fresh herbs, citrus zest, or a dash of vinegar.

Serve Immediately

Salads are best enjoyed fresh. Serve your salad as soon as it's prepared to maintain the crispness of the ingredients and the vibrancy of the flavors.

By arming yourself with the necessary equipment and following these guidelines, you'll be well on your way to creating salads that are not only healthful but also tasty and visually appealing. With enough effort, you'll discover that preparing salads can be both creative and enjoyable. Enjoy the process and experiment with various components and ways!

Classic Green Salads

Simple Caesar Salad

🍽️ 4 SERVINGS ⏱️ 15 MINUTES 🕐 10 MINUTES

Ingredients:

- 1 large head Romaine lettuce, chopped
- 1/2 cup grated Parmesan cheese
- 1 cup croutons
- 1/4 cup Caesar dressing
- 2 tbsp lemon juice
- 2 cloves garlic, minced
- Salt and pepper to taste
- Optional: grilled chicken breast, sliced

Directions:

1. Prepare the Lettuce: Wash and chop the Romaine lettuce into bite-sized pieces. Drain well and place in a large salad bowl.
2. Add Parmesan and Croutons: Sprinkle the grated Parmesan cheese and croutons over the lettuce.
3. Prepare Dressing: In a small mixing bowl, combine the Caesar dressing, lemon juice, minced garlic, and salt and pepper. Mix well.
4. Dress the Salad: Drizzle the dressing over the salad and toss till every component is equally covered.
5. Optional: Top with slices of grilled chicken breast for added protein.
6. Serve Immediately: Divide the salad into 4 serving bowls and enjoy promptly.

Nutritional Information:

Calories: 200, Protein: 7g, Carbohydrates: 13g, Fat: 14g, Fiber: 3g, Cholesterol: 10mg, Sodium: 450mg, Potassium: 300mg

Mixed Greens With Lemon Vinaigrette

🍽️ 4 SERVINGS ⏱️ 10 MINUTES 🕐 0 MINUTES

Ingredients:

- 6 cups Mixed Baby Greens
- 1/2 cup Cherry Tomatoes, halved
- 1/4 cup Red Onion, thinly sliced
- 1/4 cup Cucumber, thinly sliced
- 1/4 cup Feta Cheese, crumbled
- 1/4 cup Olive Oil
- 2 tbsp Fresh Lemon Juice
- 1 tsp Dijon Mustard
- 1 tsp Honey
- Salt and Pepper to taste

Directions:

1. Wash and dry the mixed baby greens.
2. Combine in a big salad dish the mixed greens, cherry tomatoes, red onion, cucumber, and feta cheese.
3. Whisk in a small bowl the olive oil, Dijon mustard, lemon juice, honey, salt, and pepper until well blended.
4. Drizzle the salad with the lemon vinaigrette; then, gently toss to cover everything uniformly.
5. Serve immediately.

Nutritional Information:

Calories: 180, Protein: 3g, Carbohydrates: 7g, Fat: 16g, Fiber: 2g, Cholesterol: 8mg, Sodium: 220mg, Potassium: 200mg

Spinach And Strawberry Salad

4 SERVINGS **15 MINUTES** **0 MINUTES**

Ingredients:

- 6 cups fresh baby spinach
- 2 cups sliced fresh strawberries
- 1/4 cup sliced almonds, toasted
- 1/4 cup crumbled feta cheese
- 2 tablespoons red onion, thinly sliced
- 1/4 cup balsamic vinaigrette dressing

Directions:

1. Rinse and pat dry the baby spinach leaves and the strawberries.
2. Hull and slice the strawberries evenly.
3. In a salad bowl, combine the spinach, strawberries, sliced almonds, crumbled feta cheese, and red onion.
4. Drizzle the balsamic vinaigrette dressing over the salad.
5. Toss gently to coat all the ingredients evenly with the dressing.
6. Serve immediately and enjoy!

Nutritional Information:

Calories: 160, Protein: 4g, Carbohydrates: 12g, Fat: 11g, Fiber: 3g, Cholesterol: 10mg, Sodium: 180mg, Potassium: 500mg

Arugula And Parmesan Salad

4 SERVINGS **10 MINUTES** **0 MINUTES**

Ingredients:

- 5 cups Arugula
- 1/2 cup Parmesan cheese, shaved
- 1/4 cup Extra virgin olive oil
- 2 tablespoons Fresh lemon juice
- 1 teaspoon Lemon zest
- 1/4 teaspoon Freshly ground black pepper
- 1/4 teaspoon Sea salt
- 1 clove Garlic, minced

Directions:

1. Rinse and dry the arugula thoroughly.
2. In a mixing bowl, combine the arugula and shaved Parmesan cheese.
3. Whisk together in a small bowl fresh lemon juice, extra virgin olive oil, lemon zest, freshly ground black pepper, sea salt, and chopped garlic.
4. Drizzle the dressing over the arugula and Parmesan cheese.
5. To equally cover all the elements with the dressing, gently toss the salad.
6. Present right away as an interesting side dish or appetizer.

Nutritional Information:

Calories: 180, Protein: 4g, Carbohydrates: 4g, Fat: 16g, Fiber: 1g, Cholesterol: 5mg, Sodium: 220mg, Potassium: 200mg

Garden Salad With Ranch Dressing

🍽 4 SERVINGS   ⏱ 15 MINUTES   🕐 0 MINUTES

Ingredients:

- 6 cups mixed salad greens (spinach, lettuce, arugula, etc.)
- 1 cup cherry tomatoes, halved
- 1/2 cucumber, thinly sliced
- 1/4 red onion, thinly sliced
- 1/2 cup shredded carrots
- 1/4 cup sliced radishes
- 1/2 cup croutons
- 1/4 cup shredded cheddar cheese
- 1/2 cup prepared ranch dressing

Directions:

1. Prepare the Salad Base: In a large salad bowl, combine the mixed salad greens.
2. Add Vegetables: Add the cherry tomatoes, cucumber, red onion, shredded carrots, and radishes.
3. Top with Croutons and Cheese: Sprinkle the croutons and shredded cheddar cheese evenly over the salad.
4. Dress the Salad: Drizzle the prepared ranch dressing over the top of the salad.
5. Toss and Serve: Gently toss the salad to combine all the ingredients thoroughly. Serve immediately.

Nutritional Information:

Calories: 180, Protein: 4g, Carbohydrates: 18g, Fat: 10g, Fiber: 3g, Cholesterol: 10mg, Sodium: 320mg, Potassium: 420mg

Kale And Apple Salad

🍽 4 SERVINGS   ⏱ 15 MINUTES   🕐 0 MINUTES

Ingredients:

- 4 cups kale, chopped
- 1 large apple, thinly sliced
- ¼ cup red onion, thinly sliced
- ¼ cup walnuts, chopped
- ¼ cup feta cheese, crumbled
- 2 tbsp olive oil
- 1 tbsp apple cider vinegar
- 1 tbsp honey
- 1 tsp Dijon mustard
- Salt and pepper to taste

Directions:

1. Rinse the kale thoroughly and chop into bite-sized pieces. Place in a large salad bowl.
2. Thinly slice the apple and red onion then toss them into the kale bowl.
3. Add the chopped walnuts and crumbled feta cheese to the bowl.
4. Whisk together in a small mixing bowl olive oil, apple cider vinegar, honey, and Dijon mustard until well blended. Taste-wise, add salt and pepper.
5. Drizzle the dressing over the salad and toss until the kale and other components coat evenly.
6. Serve immediately and enjoy!

Nutritional Information:

Calories: 220, Protein: 5g, Carbohydrates: 20g, Fat: 15g, Fiber: 4g, Cholesterol: 10 mg, Sodium: 220 mg, Potassium: 400 mg

Butter Lettuce With Herbs

4 SERVINGS | **15 MINUTES** | **0 MINUTES**

Ingredients:

- 1 large head Butter Lettuce, torn into bite-sized pieces
- 1/4 cup fresh Parsley, chopped
- 1/4 cup fresh Dill, chopped
- 1/4 cup fresh Basil, chopped
- 1/4 cup fresh Chives, chopped
- 1/4 cup extra virgin Olive Oil
- 2 tbsp Lemon Juice
- 1 tbsp White Wine Vinegar
- 1 tsp Dijon Mustard
- Salt and Pepper to taste

Directions:

1. Combine the torn butter lettuce, parsley, dill, basil, and chives in a large mixing bowl.
2. In a small bowl, whisk together the olive oil, lemon juice, white wine vinegar, Dijon mustard, salt, and pepper until well combined to make the dressing.
3. Drizzle the dressing over the salad ingredients then gently toss to evenly coat everything.
4. Serve immediately on chilled plates for optimal freshness.

Nutritional Information:

Calories: 150, Protein: 1g, Carbohydrates: 2g, Fat: 14g, Fiber: 1g, Cholesterol: 0 mg, Sodium: 60 mg, Potassium: 200 mg

Classic Cobb Salad

4 SERVINGS | **20 MINUTES** | **10 MINUTES**

Ingredients:

- 6 cups mixed greens (such as romaine, watercress, endive)
- 2 cups cooked chicken breast, diced
- 4 slices bacon, cooked and crumbled
- 2 large hard-boiled eggs, diced
- 1 large avocado, diced
- 2 medium tomatoes, diced
- 1/2 cup blue cheese, crumbled
- 2 tbsp chives, chopped
- 1/4 cup red wine vinegar
- 1/2 cup olive oil
- 1 tsp Dijon mustard
- Salt and pepper to taste

Directions:

1. Prepare the dressing: Whisk in a small bowl the red wine vinegar, olive oil, Dijon mustard, salt, and pepper until emulsified. Save aside.
2. Arrange the greens: Spread the mixed greens evenly on a large serving platter or in individual salad bowls.
3. Add the toppings: Arrange the diced chicken breast, crumbled bacon, hard-boiled eggs, avocado, tomatoes, blue cheese, and chives in rows on top of the greens.
4. Serve the salad: Drizzle the dressing over the salad right before serving or serve the dressing on the side for guests to add themselves.
5. Enjoy: Toss gently if desired and enjoy your Classic Cobb Salad.

Nutritional Information:

Calories: 450, Protein: 30g, Carbohydrates: 10g, Fat: 35g, Fiber: 5g, Cholesterol: 200mg, Sodium: 700mg, Potassium: 800mg

Baby Greens With Balsamic Vinaigrette

| 4 SERVINGS | 10 MINUTES | 0 MINUTES |

Ingredients:

- 6 cups Baby Greens (such as spinach, arugula, and mixed baby lettuces)
- 1/2 cup Cherry Tomatoes, halved
- 1/4 Red Onion, thinly sliced
- 1/4 cup Crumbled Feta Cheese
- 1/4 cup Sliced Almonds, toasted
- For the Balsamic Vinaigrette: 3 tablespoons Balsamic Vinegar, 1 teaspoon Dijon Mustard, one teaspoon Honey or Maple Syrup, 1/3 cup Extra Virgin Olive Oil, Salt and Black Pepper, to taste

Directions:

1. Combine in a big salad dish the baby greens, cherry tomatoes, red onion, feta cheese, and sliced almonds.
2. Combine the balsamic vinegar, Dijon mustard, honey, a bit of salt and black pepper in a small dish or jar with a tight-fitting lid. Whisk or shake until well combined.
3. Drizzle the olive oil gradually into the vinegar mixture; whisk constantly until the vinaigrette emulsifies.
4. Pour the balsamic vinaigrette over the salad just before serving. Toss gently to combine and ensure the greens are evenly coated.
5. Present right away, topped if preferred with more black pepper.

Nutritional Information:

Calories: 200, Protein: 5g, Carbohydrates: 11g, Fat: 17g, Fiber: 3g, Cholesterol: 10mg, Sodium: 220mg, Potassium: 450mg

Romaine And Radish Salad

| 4 SERVINGS | 15 MINUTES | 0 MINUTES |

Ingredients:

- 1 head Romaine lettuce, chopped
- 1 cup radishes, thinly sliced
- 1/2 cup red onion, thinly sliced
- 1/4 cup fresh parsley, chopped
- 1/4 cup freshly grated Parmesan cheese
- 1/4 cup extra virgin olive oil
- 2 tbsp lemon juice
- 1 tsp Dijon mustard
- Salt and pepper to taste

Directions:

1. In a large mixing bowl, combine the chopped Romaine lettuce, thinly sliced radishes, and thinly sliced red onion.
2. Add the chopped parsley and freshly grated Parmesan cheese to the bowl. Toss gently to combine.
3. Whisk together in a small bowl the extra virgin olive oil, lemon juice, and Dijon mustard until thoroughly blended.
4. Drizzle the dressing over the salad ingredients; then, gently but thoroughly toss to cover everything equally.
5. Taste for salt and pepper will help you season.
6. For a crisper texture, serve straight away or chill in the refrigerator for up to half an hour before.

Nutritional Information:

Calories: 160, Protein: 3g, Carbohydrates: 6g, Fat: 14g, Fiber: 2g, Cholesterol: 4mg, Sodium: 180mg, Potassium: 310mg

Green Bean And Almond Salad

4 SERVINGS   15 MINUTES   5 MINUTES

Ingredients:

- One pound fresh green beans, halved and trimmed.
- 1/4 cup slivered almonds
- 1/4 cup red onion, thinly sliced
- 2 tbsp olive oil
- 1 tbsp fresh lemon juice
- 1 tsp Dijon mustard
- 1 clove garlic, minced
- Salt and pepper, to taste

Directions:

1. One should bring a salted water kettle to boiling point. Cook the green beans, about three to five minutes, until tender-crisp. To stop the cooking, drain and plunge right into a bowl of icy water. Sort and pat dry.
2. In a small skillet over medium heat, roast the almonds to golden brown about three minutes, rotating regularly to prevent burning. Turn off the heat and reserve.
3. Whisk olive oil, lemon juice, Dijon mustard, minced salt, garlic, and pepper in a small bowl.
4. Put the green beans, red onion, roasted almonds in a large bowl.
5. Drizzle the dressing over the salad; then, toss to well blend.
6. Serve immediately away or chilled in the refrigerator for up to two hours before to have a more refreshing taste.

Nutritional Information:

Calories: 150, Protein: 3g, Carbohydrates: 9g, Fat: 11g, Fiber: 4g, Cholesterol: 0mg, Sodium: 60mg, Potassium: 225mg

Watercress And Avocado Salad

4 SERVINGS   10 MINUTES   0 MINUTES

Ingredients:

- 4 cups fresh watercress, washed and trimmed
- 2 ripe avocados, peeled, pitted, and sliced
- 1 small red onion, thinly sliced
- 1/4 cup cherry tomatoes, halved
- 2 tbsp olive oil
- 1 tbsp lemon juice
- 1 tsp Dijon mustard
- Salt and pepper, to taste
- 1 tbsp chopped fresh chives (optional)

Directions:

1. In a large salad bowl, place the fresh watercress.
2. Arrange the avocado slices, red onion, and cherry tomatoes on top of the watercress.
3. Whisk together in a small bowl olive oil, lemon juice, Dijon mustard, salt, and pepper.
4. Drizzle the salad with the dressing; then, gently toss to mix.
5. Garnish with chopped fresh chives, if desired. Serve immediately.

Nutritional Information:

Calories: 220, Protein: 3g, Carbohydrates: 12g, Fat: 20g, Fiber: 7g, Cholesterol: 0mg, Sodium: 50mg, Potassium: 750mg

Endive And Orange Salad

4 SERVINGS   **15 MINUTES**   **0 MINUTES**

Ingredients:

- 4 heads of Belgian endive, chopped
- 2 large oranges, peeled and segmented
- 1/2 cup thinly sliced red onion
- 1/4 cup toasted walnuts, chopped
- 1/4 cup crumbled goat cheese
- 1/4 cup extra-virgin olive oil
- 2 tablespoons white wine vinegar
- 1 tablespoon honey
- Salt and pepper to taste

Directions:

1. Combine the chopped endive, orange sections and red onion in a big salad dish.
2. To make the dressing, whisk together in a small bowl the olive oil, white wine vinegar, honey, salt, and pepper.
3. Drizzle the dressing over the salad then gently toss to mix.
4. Over the salad, scatter the toasted walnuts and crumbled goat cheese.
5. Present straight away.

Nutritional Information:

Calories: 220, Protein: 4g, Carbohydrates: 18g, Fat: 16g, Fiber: 4g, Cholesterol: 7mg, Sodium: 170mg, Potassium: 450mg

Bibb Lettuce With Dijon Dressing

4 SERVINGS   **15 MINUTES**   **0 MINUTES**

Ingredients:

- 1 head Bibb lettuce, washed and torn into bite-sized pieces
- ¼ cup extra-virgin olive oil
- 2 tablespoons Dijon mustard
- 1 tablespoon red wine vinegar
- 1 clove garlic, minced
- Salt and pepper, to taste
- 1 small shallot, thinly sliced
- ¼ cup crumbled feta cheese (optional)
- 2 tablespoons chopped fresh chives (optional)

Directions:

1. To make the dressing, whisk together in a small bowl the extra-virgin olive oil, Dijon mustard, red wine vinegar, minced garlic, salt, and pepper until well mixed.
2. In a large salad bowl, place the torn Bibb lettuce.
3. Pour the Dijon dressing over the lettuce and gently toss to coat the leaves evenly.
4. Add the thinly sliced shallot to the salad and toss again.
5. If using, sprinkle the crumbled feta cheese and chopped fresh chives over the top of the salad.
6. Serve immediately and enjoy.

Nutritional Information:

Calories: 150, Protein: 2g, Carbohydrates: 3g, Fat: 14g, Fiber: 1g, Cholesterol: 0mg, Sodium: 190mg, Potassium: 180mg

Cucumber And Mint Salad

4 SERVINGS — **10 MINUTES** — **0 MINUTES**

Ingredients:

- 2 large cucumbers, thinly sliced
- 1/4 cup fresh mint leaves, finely chopped
- 1/4 cup red onion, thinly sliced
- 1 tablespoon olive oil
- 1 tablespoon lemon juice
- 1/2 teaspoon salt
- 1/4 teaspoon black pepper

Directions:

1. In a large bowl, combine the thinly sliced cucumbers, chopped fresh mint leaves, and thinly sliced red onion.
2. Whisk together in a small bowl olive oil, lemon juice, salt, and black pepper.
3. Drizzle the dressing over the cucumber combination and carefully toss to guarantee equal coating of all the components.
4. To let the tastes marry, let the salad sit for roughly five minutes.
5. Serve immediately or refrigerate for up to 1 hour to chill before serving.

Nutritional Information:

Calories: 65, Protein: 1g, Carbohydrates: 7g, Fat: 4g, Fiber: 1g, Cholesterol: 0 mg, Sodium: 300 mg, Potassium: 200 mg

Beet And Goat Cheese Salad

4 SERVINGS — **15 MINUTES**

Ingredients:

- 4 medium beets
- 4 oz goat cheese, crumbled
- 1/4 cup chopped walnuts
- 5 oz mixed greens
- 2 tbsp olive oil
- 1 tbsp balsamic vinegar
- 1 tsp honey
- Salt and pepper to taste

Directions:

1. Turn on the oven to 400°F (200°C). Wrap every beet in aluminum foil then lay on a baking pan. Roast in the oven for 45 minutes, or until a fork inserted into the beets comes out clean. Let to cool.
2. Peel off the skins once the beets cool, then cut into bite-sized bits.
3. To make the dressing, whirl olive oil, balsamic vinegar, salt, honey, and pepper in a small bowl.
4. Combine the mixed greens, diced beets, shredded goat cheese, walnuts in a big salad bowl.
5. Drizzle the salad with the dressing; then, toss to evenly coat.
6. Present immediately and savor!

Nutritional Information:

Calories: 250, Protein: 7g, Carbohydrates: 22g, Fat: 17g, Fiber: 5g, Cholesterol: 10mg, Sodium: 200mg, Potassium: 600mg

Crunchy Veggie Salads

Carrot And Raisin Salad

4 SERVINGS 15 MINUTES 0 MINUTES

Ingredients:

- 4 cups shredded carrots
- 1 cup raisins
- 1/2 cup plain Greek yogurt (or you can use mayonnaise for a richer dressing)
- 2 tbsp honey
- 1 tbsp lemon juice
- 1/4 tsp salt
- 1/4 tsp black pepper
- 1/4 cup chopped walnuts (optional, for extra crunch)

Directions:

1. Combine the shred carrots and raisins in a large bowl. Whisk in a separate smaller bowl the Greek yogurt (or mayonnaise), honey, lemon juice, salt, and black pepper until smooth.
2. Pour the dressing over the carrot and raisin mixture. Toss well to combine, ensuring all ingredients are evenly coated.
3. If adding walnuts for extra crunch, sprinkle them over the salad and gently mix in.
4. Present right away or chill for around one hour to let the flavors marry.

Nutritional Information:

Calories: 180, Protein: 3g, Carbohydrates: 40g, Fat: 4g, Fiber: 5g, Cholesterol: 5mg, Sodium: 190mg, Potassium: 510mg

Classic Coleslaw

6 SERVINGS 15 MINUTES 0 MINUTES

Ingredients:

- 1 medium head of green cabbage, finely shredded
- 1 large carrot, peeled and grated
- 1/2 cup mayonnaise
- 2 tablespoons apple cider vinegar
- 1 tablespoon Dijon mustard
- 1 tablespoon honey
- 1/2 teaspoon celery seed
- Salt and pepper to taste

Directions:

1. Combine the finely shredded cabbage and grated carrot in a big mixing dish. Whisk in a separate small bowl the mayonnaise, apple cider vinegar, Dijon mustard, honey, salt, celery seed, and pepper until smooth and well combined.
2. Drizzle the dressing over a cabbage and carrot combo. Till the dressing coats the vegetables equally, toss everything together.
3. To let the tastes marry, cover the bowl and chill for at least one hour before serving.
4. Serve cold, topped with a sprinkle of extra celery seed if desired.

Nutritional Information:

Calories: 150, Protein: 1g, Carbohydrates: 9g, Fat: 13g, Fiber: 2g, Cholesterol: 10mg, Sodium: 220mg, Potassium: 270mg

Asian Slaw With Peanut Dressing

🍽 4 SERVINGS ⏱ 20 MINUTES 🕐 0 MINUTES

Ingredients:

- 4 cups shredded cabbage
- 1 cup shredded carrots
- 1 bell pepper, thinly sliced
- 1/2 cup chopped fresh cilantro
- 1/2 cup sliced green onions
- 1/2 cup chopped peanuts
- 1/4 cup peanut butter
- 2 tablespoons soy sauce
- 2 tablespoons rice vinegar
- 1 tablespoon honey
- 1 tablespoon lime juice
- 1 teaspoon sesame oil
- 1-2 tablespoons water (to thin the dressing, if necessary)

Directions:

1. Combine in a big bowl the chopped fresh cilantro, shredded cabbage, shredded carrots, thinly sliced bell pepper, and sliced green onions.
2. Whisk in a small bowl the peanut butter, rice vinegar, soy sauce, honey, lime juice, sesame oil. Add water one tablespoon at a time until the dressing gets your desired consistency if it is too thick.
3. Pour the peanut dressing over the vegetable mixture and toss well to coat.
4. Sprinkle the chopped peanuts on top of the salad and toss lightly to distribute.
5. Serve immediately, or refrigerate for up to 2 hours to let the flavors meld.

Nutritional Information:

Calories: 210, Protein: 6g, Carbohydrates: 18g, Fat: 14g, Fiber: 5g, Cholesterol: 0mg, Sodium: 320mg, Potassium: 450mg

Cucumber And Tomato Salad

🍽 4 SERVINGS ⏱ 10 MINUTES 🕐 0 MINUTES

Ingredients:

- 2 large cucumbers, sliced
- 3 large tomatoes, diced
- 1/2 red onion, thinly sliced
- 1/4 cup fresh parsley, chopped
- 2 tbsp olive oil
- 1 tbsp red wine vinegar
- Salt and pepper, to taste

Directions:

1. Combine the sliced cucumbers, chopped tomatoes, and thinly sliced red onion in a big bowl.
2. To the bowl add the chopped fresh parsley and stir everything together.
3. Drizzle over the salad mix the olive oil and red wine vinegar.
4. Taste should guide the season with salt and pepper.
5. Toss everything till nicely blended.
6. For best taste, refrigerate till one hour before serving or serve straight away.

Nutritional Information:

Calories: 90, Protein: 2g, Carbohydrates: 13g, Fat: 5g, Fiber: 3g, Cholesterol: 0 mg, Sodium: 20 mg, Potassium: 450 mg

Broccoli And Cheddar Salad

4 SERVINGS   15 MINUTES   0 MINUTES

Ingredients:

- 3 cups fresh broccoli florets
- 1 cup shredded cheddar cheese
- 1/2 cup red onion, finely chopped
- 1/4 cup dried cranberries
- 1/4 cup sunflower seeds
- 1/2 cup mayonnaise
- 2 tablespoons apple cider vinegar
- 1 tablespoon honey
- Salt and pepper to taste

Directions:

1. In a large mixing bowl, combine the broccoli florets, shredded cheddar cheese, chopped red onion, dried cranberries, and sunflower seeds.
2. In a small bowl, whisk together the mayonnaise, apple cider vinegar, honey, salt, and pepper until well blended.
3. Pour the dressing over the broccoli mixture and toss to coat all ingredients evenly.
4. Refrigerate the salad for at least 30 minutes before serving to allow the flavors to meld together.
5. Serve chilled and enjoy!

Nutritional Information:

Calories: 310, Protein: 8g, Carbohydrates: 17g, Fat: 25g, Fiber: 3g, Cholesterol: 15mg, Sodium: 310mg, Potassium: 458mg

Jicama And Citrus Salad

4 SERVINGS   20 MINUTES   0 MINUTES

Ingredients:

- 2 cups jicama, peeled and julienned
- 1 orange, peeled and segmented
- 1 grapefruit, peeled and segmented
- 1 lime, juiced
- 1 tablespoon honey
- 1/4 cup red onion, thinly sliced
- 1/4 cup fresh cilantro, chopped
- 1/4 teaspoon salt
- 1/8 teaspoon black pepper
- 1 tablespoon olive oil

Directions:

1. In a large mixing bowl, combine the julienned jicama, orange segments, and grapefruit segments.
2. In a small bowl, whisk together the lime juice, honey, salt, pepper, and olive oil to create the dressing.
3. Pour the dressing over the jicama and citrus mixture.
4. Add the thinly sliced red onion and fresh cilantro to the bowl.
5. Toss all ingredients together until the salad is evenly coated with the dressing.
6. Serve immediately or refrigerate for up to 1 hour to allow the flavors to meld.

Nutritional Information:

Calories: 110, Protein: 1g, Carbohydrates: 27g, Fat: 3g, Fiber: 5g, Cholesterol: 0 mg, Sodium: 150 mg, Potassium: 380 mg

Crunchy Radish Salad

4 SERVINGS | **15 MINUTES** | **0 MINUTES**

Ingredients:
- 1 cup radishes, thinly sliced
- 1 cup cucumber, diced
- 1/2 cup red bell pepper, diced
- 1/4 cup red onion, thinly sliced
- 1/4 cup fresh parsley, chopped
- 2 tbsp olive oil
- 1 tbsp lemon juice
- 1/2 tsp sea salt
- 1/4 tsp black pepper
- 1/4 cup sunflower seeds

Directions:
1. In a large bowl, combine the thinly sliced radishes, diced cucumber, diced red bell pepper, and thinly sliced red onion.
2. Add the chopped parsley to the vegetable mix.
3. In a small bowl, whisk together the olive oil, lemon juice, sea salt, and black pepper until well combined.
4. Pour the dressing over the mixed vegetables and toss to coat evenly.
5. Sprinkle the sunflower seeds over the salad and gently mix to incorporate.
6. Serve immediately or refrigerate for 10 minutes to allow flavors to meld.

Nutritional Information:
Calories: 120 kcal, Protein: 2g, Carbohydrates: 6g, Fat: 10g, Fiber: 2g, Cholesterol: 0 mg, Sodium: 310 mg, Potassium: 280 mg

Bell Pepper And Corn Salad

4 SERVINGS | **20 MINUTES** | **0 MINUTES**

Ingredients:
- 2 large bell peppers (preferably one red and one yellow), diced
- 1 cup fresh or canned corn kernels, drained if using canned
- 1/2 red onion, finely chopped
- 1 cup cherry tomatoes, halved
- 1/4 cup fresh cilantro, chopped
- 2 tablespoons olive oil
- 1 tablespoon freshly squeezed lime juice
- 1 teaspoon salt (adjust to taste)
- 1/2 teaspoon black pepper
- 1/2 teaspoon ground cumin (optional)
- 1 avocado, diced (optional, for added creaminess)
- 1 jalapeño, finely chopped (optional, for added heat)

Directions:
1. In a large mixing bowl, combine the diced bell peppers, corn kernels, finely chopped red onion, and halved cherry tomatoes.
2. Add the chopped fresh cilantro to the bowl and mix well to distribute the ingredients evenly.
3. In a small bowl, whisk together the olive oil, freshly squeezed lime juice, salt, black pepper, and ground cumin (if using).
4. Pour the dressing over the salad and toss gently until all the vegetables are well coated.
5. If using, fold in the diced avocado and finely chopped jalapeño into the salad.
6. Taste and adjust seasoning as needed.
7. Let the salad sit for at least 10 minutes before serving to allow the flavors to meld together.

Nutritional Information:
Calories: 150, Protein: 3g, Carbohydrates: 20g, Fat: 8g, Fiber: 5g, Cholesterol: 0mg, Sodium: 370mg, Potassium: 400mg

Zucchini Ribbon Salad

4 SERVINGS   15 MINUTES

Ingredients:

- 2 medium zucchinis
- 1 cup cherry tomatoes, halved
- 1/4 cup red onion, thinly sliced
- 1/4 cup fresh basil leaves, torn
- 1/4 cup crumbled feta cheese
- 2 tablespoons extra virgin olive oil
- 1 tablespoon lemon juice
- 1/2 teaspoon salt
- 1/4 teaspoon freshly ground black pepper

Directions:

1. Use a vegetable peeler or mandoline to slice the zucchinis into thin ribbons.
2. Place the zucchini ribbons in a large salad bowl.
3. Add the halved cherry tomatoes, thinly sliced red onion, torn basil leaves, and crumbled feta cheese to the bowl.
4. In a small bowl, whisk together the extra virgin olive oil, lemon juice, salt, and freshly ground black pepper.
5. Pour the dressing over the salad and gently toss to combine.
6. Serve immediately or refrigerate for up to 30 minutes before serving to let the flavors meld.

Nutritional Information:

Calories: 110, Protein: 3g, Carbohydrates: 6g, Fat: 9g, Fiber: 2g, Cholesterol: 10mg, Sodium: 300mg, Potassium: 400mg

Rainbow Slaw With Lime Dressing

4 SERVINGS   15 MINUTES   0 MINUTES

Ingredients:

- 2 cups red cabbage, thinly sliced
- 2 cups green cabbage, thinly sliced
- 1 cup carrots, shredded
- 1 red bell pepper, thinly sliced
- 1 yellow bell pepper, thinly sliced
- 1/2 cup fresh cilantro, chopped
- 1/4 cup green onions, chopped
- 2 tbsp lime juice
- 1 tbsp apple cider vinegar
- 1 tbsp honey
- 2 tbsp olive oil
- Salt and pepper to taste

Directions:

1. In a large bowl, combine red cabbage, green cabbage, carrots, red bell pepper, yellow bell pepper, cilantro, and green onions.
2. In a small bowl, whisk together lime juice, apple cider vinegar, honey, olive oil, salt, and pepper.
3. Pour the lime dressing over the slaw mixture and toss to coat thoroughly.
4. Allow the slaw to sit for 10 minutes to let the flavors meld together.
5. Serve immediately or refrigerate for later use.

Nutritional Information:

Calories: 110, Protein: 2g, Carbohydrates: 15g, Fat: 6g, Fiber: 4g, Cholesterol: 0mg, Sodium: 68mg, Potassium: 370mg

Marinated Mushroom Salad

4 SERVINGS   15 MINUTES   10 MINUTES

Ingredients:

- 1 lb (450g) button mushrooms, halved
- 1/4 cup olive oil
- 3 tbsp balsamic vinegar
- 2 cloves garlic, minced
- 1/2 tsp dried oregano
- 1/4 tsp salt
- 1/4 tsp black pepper
- 1/2 red onion, thinly sliced
- 1/4 cup fresh parsley, chopped

Directions:

1. In a large saucepan, bring lightly salted water to a boil.
2. Put the halved mushrooms in the boiling water and simmer for five minutes, until just tender.
3. Drain the mushrooms and set aside to cool.
4. Whisk in a big mixing basin the olive oil, balsamic vinegar, minced garlic, dried oregano, salt, and black pepper.
5. Add the cooled mushrooms, thinly sliced red onion, and chopped parsley to the dressing.
6. Toss all ingredients together until mushrooms and onions are evenly coated with the marinade.
7. Cover the bowl and chill for at least one hour to let the tastes marry.
8. Toss the salad again before serving.

Nutritional Information:

Calories: 150, Protein: 3g, Carbohydrates: 10g, Fat: 12g, Fiber: 2g, Cholesterol: 0mg, Sodium: 150mg, Potassium: 430mg

Cabbage And Apple Slaw

4 SERVINGS   15 MINUTES   0 MINUTES

Ingredients:

- 4 cups shredded green cabbage
- 1 large apple, julienned (Granny Smith or Honeycrisp recommended)
- 1 medium carrot, grated
- 1/4 cup thinly sliced red onion
- 1/4 cup chopped fresh parsley
- 1/4 cup apple cider vinegar
- 2 tablespoons olive oil
- 1 tablespoon honey
- 1 tablespoon Dijon mustard
- Salt and pepper to taste

Directions:

1. Combine in a big bowl shredded cabbage, julienned apple, grated carrot, sliced red onion, and chopped parsley.
2. Whisk in a small bowl the apple cider vinegar, olive oil, honey, Dijon mustard, salt, and pepper until well blended.
3. Drizzle the dressing over the cabbage mixture, then toss carefully to cover everything.
4. Before serving, let the slaw sit for at least ten minutes so the flavors marry. Present either chilled or room temperature.

Nutritional Information:

Calories: 120, Protein: 1g, Carbohydrates: 19g, Fat: 5g, Fiber: 4g, Cholesterol: 0mg, Sodium: 60mg, Potassium: 250mg

Snap Pea And Radish Salad

🍽️ 4 SERVINGS ⏱️ 15 MINUTES 🕐 0 MINUTES

Ingredients:

- 2 cups snap peas, trimmed and halved
- 6 radishes, thinly sliced
- 1/4 cup red onion, thinly sliced
- 1 tbsp fresh dill, chopped
- 2 tbsp olive oil
- 1 tbsp lemon juice
- 1 tsp Dijon mustard
- 1/2 tsp honey
- Salt and pepper to taste

Directions:

1. Combine in a big bowl the snap peas, radishes, red onion, and fresh dill.
2. Whisk together in a small bowl olive oil, lemon juice, Dijon mustard, honey, salt, and pepper until well blended.
3. Drizzle the dressing over the vegetables then mix to evenly coat.
4. Taste and adjust with more salt and pepper as necessary.
5. To allow the flavors mingle, serve right away or chill for up to two hours..

Nutritional Information:

Calories: 110, Protein: 2g, Carbohydrates: 8g, Fat: 7g, Fiber: 3g, Cholesterol: 0 mg, Sodium: 60 mg, Potassium: 220 mg

Spicy Kimchi Slaw

🍽️ 4 SERVINGS ⏱️ 15 MINUTES 🕐 0 MINUTES

Ingredients:

- 2 cups shredded napa cabbage
- 1 cup julienned carrots
- 1 cup thinly sliced radishes
- 1/2 cup chopped green onions
- 1 cup kimchi, chopped
- 1/4 cup kimchi juice (from the kimchi jar)
- 2 tablespoons rice vinegar
- 1 tablespoon soy sauce
- 1 tablespoon sesame oil
- 1 tablespoon honey
- 1 teaspoon gochujang (Korean chili paste)
- 1 teaspoon toasted sesame seeds

Directions:

1. Combine in a big bowl the shredded napa cabbage, julienned carrots, thinly sliced radishes, and chopped green onions.
2. Add the chopped kimchi and toss to evenly distribute.
3. In a small bowl, whisk together the kimchi juice, rice vinegar, soy sauce, sesame oil, honey, and gochujang until well blended.
4. Drizzle the dressing over the vegetable mixture and toss carefully to cover everything.
5. Sprinkle toasted sesame seeds on top before serving.
6. To let the flavors mingle, serve right away or chill for up to two hours.

Nutritional Information:

Calories: 90, Protein: 1.5g, Carbohydrates: 11g, Fat: 5g, Fiber: 3g, Cholesterol: 0mg, Sodium: 540mg, Potassium: 300mg

Carrot And Beet Salad

4 SERVINGS   **15 MINUTES**   **0 MINUTES**

Ingredients:

- 2 medium carrots, julienned
- 2 medium beets, peeled and julienned
- 1 small red onion, thinly sliced
- 3 tablespoons chopped fresh parsley
- 2 tablespoons olive oil
- 1 tablespoon apple cider vinegar
- 1 tablespoon lemon juice
- 1/2 teaspoon salt
- 1/4 teaspoon black pepper
- 1/4 cup chopped walnuts (optional)

Directions:

1. In a big basin, toss the julienned beets and carrots.
2. To the bowl including the carrots and beets, toss the chopped fresh parsley and thinly sliced red onion.
3. Whisk together in a bowl olive oil, lemon juice, salt, apple cider vinegar, and black pepper until well blended.
4. Drizzle the dressing over the salad mix and toss until every vegetable is uniformly covered.
5. For an extra crunch, top the salad with the chopped walnuts, if using.
6. To let the tastes marry, serve right away or chill for up to two hours.

Nutritional Information:

Calories: 180, Protein: 3g, Carbohydrates: 20g, Fat: 11g, Fiber: 5g, Cholesterol: 0mg, Sodium: 310mg, Potassium: 550mg

Fennel And Orange Salad

4 SERVINGS   **15 MINUTES**   **0 MINUTES**

Ingredients:

- 2 large fennel bulbs, thinly sliced
- 2 large oranges, peeled and segmented
- 1/4 cup red onion, thinly sliced
- 1/4 cup fresh parsley, chopped
- 1/4 cup pitted black olives, halved
- 2 tablespoons extra-virgin olive oil
- 1 tablespoon fresh lemon juice
- Salt and freshly ground black pepper, to taste

Directions:

1. Combine in a big salad dish the thinly sliced fennel bulbs, orange segments, red onion, parsley, and black olives.
2. Whisk fresh lemon juice and extra-virgin olive oil in a small bowl until completely blended.
3. Drizzle the dressing over the salad then gently mix to evenly coat every component.
4. Taste using fresh ground black pepper and salt to season.
5. Present right away or chill in the refrigerator for ten to fifteen minutes to let flavors marry.

Nutritional Information:

Calories: 140, Protein: 2g, Carbohydrates: 14g, Fat: 9g, Fiber: 4g, Cholesterol: 0mg, Sodium: 150mg, Potassium: 450mg

Hearty Grain and Bean Salads

Quinoa And Black Bean Salad

🍽 4 SERVINGS ⏱ 15 MINUTES 🕒 15 MINUTES

Ingredients:

- 1 cup quinoa, rinsed
- 2 cups water
- 1 can (15 ounces) black beans, drained and washed.
- 1 cup fresh or frozen, thawed corn kernels.
- 1 red bell pepper, diced
- 1/4 cup red onion, finely diced
- 1/4 cup cilantro, chopped
- 1 avocado, diced
- 1/4 cup olive oil
- 2 tablespoons lime juice
- 1 teaspoon ground cumin
- Salt and pepper to taste

Directions:

1. Put the quinoa and water in a medium sauté pan. Bring to a boil; then, decrease to a simmer; cover; cook until the quinoa is tender—about 15 minutes—that is the water absorbed. Fluff using a fork.
2. Combine in a big bowl the cooked quinoa, black beans, red bell pepper, corn, red onion, and cilantro.
3. In a little bowl olive oil, lime juice, cumin, salt, and pepper, whisk together.
4. Drizzle the dressing over the salad and stir-through.
5. Carefully fold the cubed avocado.
6. If necessary, adjust the seasoning with more pepper and salt. Present either chilled or room temperature.

Nutritional Information:

Calories: 320, Protein: 9g, Carbohydrates: 42g, Fat: 13g, Fiber: 11g, Cholesterol: 0 mg, Sodium: 380 mg, Potassium: 749 mg

Mediterranean Farro Salad

🍽 4 SERVINGS ⏱ 15 MINUTES 🕒 30 MINUTES

Ingredients:

- 1 cup Farro
- 2 cups Water
- 1/2 cup Diced Cucumbers
- 1/2 cup Halved Cherry Tomatoes
- 1/4 cup Chopped Red Onion
- 1/4 cup Diced Kalamata Olives
- 1/4 cup Crumbled Feta Cheese
- 2 tablespoons Chopped Fresh Parsley
- 2 tablespoons Extra Virgin Olive Oil
- 1 tablespoon Red Wine Vinegar
- 1 teaspoon Lemon Juice
- 1/2 teaspoon Dried Oregano
- Salt and Pepper to taste

Directions:

1. Under cold water, rinse a cup of farro.
2. Boil two cups of water in a medium pot. Add the rinsed farro; cut heat to low; cover; simmer for around half an hour or until soft. Empty any extra water, then let the farro cool.
3. Combine in a large salad dish the chilled farro, 1/2 cup sliced cucumbers, 1/2 cup halved cherry tomatoes, 1/4 cup chopped red onion, 1/4 cup diced Kalamata olives, and 1/4 cup crumbled feta cheese.
4. Whisk two tablespoons extra virgin olive oil, one tablespoon red wine vinegar, one teaspoon lemon juice, one half teaspoon dried oregano, and salt and pepper to taste in a small bowl.
5. Drizzle the dressing over the salad and stir-through.
6. Top with two tablespoons chopped fresh parsley.
7. Present right away or chill to let the tastes marry.

Nutritional Information:

Calories: 287, Protein: 8g, Carbohydrates: 36g, Fat: 12g, Fiber: 5g, Cholesterol: 10mg, Sodium: 300mg, Potassium: 300mg

Barley And Roasted Vegetable Salad

🍽 4 SERVINGS   ⏱ 20 MINUTES   🕐 40 MINUTES

Ingredients:

- 1 cup pearl barley
- 2 1/2 cups water
- 1 red bell pepper, diced
- 1 yellow bell pepper, diced
- 1 small red onion, sliced
- 1 zucchini, diced
- 2 tablespoons olive oil
- 1 teaspoon salt
- 1/2 teaspoon black pepper
- 1 teaspoon dried thyme
- 1 can (15 oz) chickpeas, rinsed and drained
- 1/4 cup chopped fresh parsley
- 1/4 cup crumbled feta cheese
- 2 tablespoons lemon juice
- 1 tablespoon red wine vinegar

Directions:

1. Set the oven for 400°F (200°C).
2. Under cold water, rince the barley. Put the barley and water in a medium saucepan. Boil first; then, lower to a simmer. Cook covered until the barley is soft, 25 to 30 minutes. Empty any extra water; then, let cool.
3. As the barley cooks, arrange the bell peppers, red onion, and zucchini on a baking pan. Drizzle olive oil; then, top with salt, black pepper, dried thyme. Toss to distribute fairly. Roast until the vegetables are soft and somewhat browned, 25 to 30 minutes in the preheated oven. Allow coolness.
4. Combine in a big bowl the roasted veggies, chickpeas, cooked barley, and parsley. toss to properly mix.
5. Whisk in a small bowl the lemon juice and red wine vinegar. Drizzle over the barley mixture and turn to coat.
6. Before serving, scatter crumbled feta cheese on the salad.

Nutritional Information:

Calories: 320, Protein: 10g, Carbohydrates: 52g, Fat: 9g, Fiber: 12g, Cholesterol: 10 mg, Sodium: 620 mg, Potassium: 600 mg

Wild Rice And Cranberry Salad

🍽 6 SERVINGS   ⏱ 20 MINUTES   🕐 45 MINUTES

Ingredients:

- 1 cup wild rice
- 3 cups water
- 1/2 cup dried cranberries
- 1/4 cup chopped pecans
- 1/4 cup chopped red onion
- 1/4 cup chopped fresh parsley
- 1/4 cup crumbled feta cheese
- 3 tbsp olive oil
- 2 tbsp apple cider vinegar
- 1 tbsp honey
- 1 tsp Dijon mustard
- Salt and pepper to taste

Directions:

1. Under cool water, rine the wild rice. In a medium saucepan set the three cups of water to boil. Add the wild rice; lower the heat to low; cover; then, simmer for roughly 45 minutes or until the rice is cooked and most of the water has absorbed. Empty any extra water; then let the rice cool.
2. Combine in a big bowl the chopped nuts, parsley, red onion, dried cranberries, and cooked wild rice.
3. Whisk together in a small bowl olive oil, honey, apple cider vinegar, and Dijon mustard. Taste-test and season with salt and pepper.
4. Drizzle the dressing over the wild rice mixture and stir-through.
5. Sort the feta cheese gently.
6. To let the tastes marry, serve right away or chill for up to two days.

Nutritional Information:

Calories: 275, Protein: 6g, Carbohydrates: 39g, Fat: 11g, Fiber: 3g, Cholesterol: 8mg, Sodium: 125mg, Potassium: 200mg

Chickpea And Cucumber Salad

4 SERVINGS | 15 MINUTES | 0 MINUTES

Ingredients:

- 2 cups canned chickpeas, drained and rinsed
- 1 large cucumber, diced
- 1 cup cherry tomatoes, halved
- 1/2 red onion, finely chopped
- 1/4 cup fresh parsley, chopped
- 1/4 cup olive oil
- 2 tablespoons lemon juice
- 1 tablespoon red wine vinegar
- 1 teaspoon dried oregano
- Salt and pepper to taste

Directions:

1. Combine in a large bowl chickpeas, chopped cucumber, cherry tomatoes, red onion, and parsley.
2. Whisk red wine vinegar, olive oil, lemon juice, then dried oregano in a small basin.
3. Dress the salad then toss to mix.
4. Taste-test and season with salt and pepper.
5. To let tastes marry, serve right now or chill for up to two hours.

Nutritional Information:

Calories: 220, Protein: 6g, Carbohydrates: 24g, Fat: 12g, Fiber: 6g, Cholesterol: 0mg, Sodium: 300mg, Potassium: 420mg

Bulgur And Parsley Salad

4 SERVINGS | 15 MINUTES | 20 MINUTES

Ingredients:

- 1 cup bulgur
- 1 ½ cups boiling water
- 1 bunch fresh parsley, chopped
- 2 medium tomatoes, diced
- 1 small cucumber, diced
- ½ cup red onion, finely chopped
- ¼ cup fresh mint leaves, chopped
- ⅓ cup olive oil
- ¼ cup fresh lemon juice
- Salt and pepper to taste

Directions:

1. Arrange the bulgur in a big bowl then pour boiling water over it. Cover and let it sit until the bulgur absorbs the water and becomes tender, perhaps 15 to 20 minutes.
2. Use a fork to fluff the bulgur so you may separate the grains.
3. Add to the bowl with the bulgur the chopped parsley, diced tomatoes, sliced cucumber, finely chopped red onion, and chopped mint leaves. thoroughly mix.
4. Whisk in a small bowl the olive oil, fresh lemon juice, salt, and pepper. Drizzle this dressing over the bulgur mixture then toss to blend.
5. To let the tastes combine, serve right away or chill for at least half an hour.

Nutritional Information:

Calories: 250, Protein: 5g, Carbohydrates: 28g, Fat: 14g, Fiber: 7g, Cholesterol: 0mg, Sodium: 50mg, Potassium: 400mg

Lentil And Feta Salad

4 SERVINGS   15 MINUTES   25 MINUTES

Ingredients:

- 1 cup dry lentils, rinsed
- 4 cups water
- 1/2 cup crumbled feta cheese
- 1 cup cherry tomatoes, halved
- 1/2 small red onion, finely chopped
- 1/4 cup chopped fresh parsley
- 3 tablespoons olive oil
- 2 tablespoons red wine vinegar
- 1 teaspoon Dijon mustard
- Salt and pepper to taste

Directions:

1. On medium saucepan set over high heat, pour the water. Add the lentils and drop the heat to a simmer. About 20 to 25 minutes, cook the lentils till soft but not mushy. Empty and let cool.
2. Arrange the cooked lentils, feta cheese, red onion, cherry tomatoes, and parsley in a big bowl.
3. Whisk together in a small bowl the olive oil, red wine vinegar, Dijon mustard, salt, and pepper until thoroughly blended.
4. Drizzle the dressing over the lentil mixture then gently toss to blend. If necessary, change seasoning with more salt and pepper.
5. For tastes to merge, serve right away or chill for up to three days.

Nutritional Information:

Calories: 280, Protein: 12g, Carbohydrates: 28g, Fat: 14g, Fiber: 12g, Cholesterol: 15 mg, Sodium: 380 mg, Potassium: 500 mg

Couscous And Tomato Salad

4 SERVINGS   15 MINUTES   10 MINUTES

Ingredients:

- 1 cup couscous
- 1 1/4 cups boiling water
- 1 cup cherry tomatoes, halved
- 1/4 cup red onion, finely chopped
- 1/4 cup fresh parsley, chopped
- 1/4 cup fresh basil, chopped
- 2 tbsp lemon juice
- 2 tbsp olive oil
- Salt and pepper to taste

Directions:

1. Add the couscuous in a big heatproof bowl.
2. Over the couscous, pour the boiling water; cover; let it rest for ten minutes.
3. Use a fork to fluff the couscous such that the grains separate.
4. To the couscous, add the cherry tomatoes, red onion, parsley, and basil; toss well.
5. Whisk together in a small bowl the lemon juice, olive oil, salt, and pepper.
6. Drizzle the dressing over the salad and stir-through.
7. If preferred, adjust seasoning with more salt and pepper.
8. To let the flavors marry before serving, refrigerate for up to two hours or serve right away.

Nutritional Information:

Calories: 220, Protein: 5g, Carbohydrates: 30g, Fat: 9g, Fiber: 3g, Cholesterol: 0mg, Sodium: 100mg, Potassium: 340mg

Brown Rice And Avocado Salad

🍽 4 SERVINGS   ⏱ 20 MINUTES   🕐 40 MINUTES

Ingredients:

- 1 cup brown rice
- 2 ripe avocados, diced
- 1 cup cherry tomatoes, halved
- 1/2 red onion, finely chopped
- 1 cup black beans, rinsed and drained
- 1/4 cup chopped fresh cilantro
- 1/4 cup lime juice (about 2 limes)
- 3 tablespoons olive oil
- 1 teaspoon cumin
- Salt and pepper to taste

Directions:

1. Follow package directions on brown rice cooking. Fluff once cooked with a fork; allow it cool to room temperature.
2. Combine in a big bowl the cooked and cooled brown rice, diced avocados, halved cherry tomatoes, finely chopped red onion, and black beans.
3. Whisk together in a small bowl olive oil, lime juice, cumin, salt, and pepper. Taste-test and adjust the seasoning.
4. To guarantee all components are well-coated, pour the dressing over the rice mixture and gently toss.
5. As garnish, toss chopped fresh cilantro in the salad.
6. Present straight away or refrigerated for up to 24 hours before serving.

Nutritional Information:

Orzo And Spinach Salad

🍽 6 SERVINGS   ⏱ 15 MINUTES   🕐 10 MINUTES

Ingredients:

- 1 cup orzo pasta
- 5 ounces baby spinach, chopped
- 1 cup cherry tomatoes, halved
- 1/4 cup red onion, finely diced
- 1/2 cup feta cheese, crumbled
- 1/4 cup Kalamata olives, pitted and sliced
- 2 tablespoons fresh parsley, chopped
- 1/4 cup extra virgin olive oil
- 2 tablespoons red wine vinegar
- 1 teaspoon Dijon mustard
- Salt and pepper, to taste

Directions:

1. Cook the orzo noodles al dente, following package directions. To halt cooking, drain and rinse under cold water. Set aside.
2. Combine in a big bowl the chopped spinach, cherry tomatoes, red onion, feta cheese, Kalamata olives, and parsley.
3. In a small bowl olive oil, Dijon mustard, red wine vinegar, salt, and pepper, whisk together until thoroughly combined.
4. Toss the cooked orzo into the big bowl with the veggies to mix.
5. Drizzle the dress over the salad; then, toss one more to ensure uniform covering.
6. If preferred, adjust the seasoning with more salt and pepper. Present either chilled or room temperature.

Nutritional Information:

Calories: 250, Protein: 7g, Carbohydrates: 25g, Fat: 14g, Fiber: 3g, Cholesterol: 15 mg, Sodium: 400 mg, Potassium: 350 mg

Three-Bean Salad

6 SERVINGS   **20 MINUTES**   **0 MINUTES**

Ingredients:

- 1 cup canned kidney beans, drained and rinsed
- 1 cup canned green beans, drained and rinsed
- 1 cup canned chickpeas, drained and rinsed
- 1/2 cup chopped red onion
- 1/2 cup diced red bell pepper
- 1/4 cup chopped fresh parsley
- 1/3 cup apple cider vinegar
- 2 tablespoons olive oil
- 1 tablespoon sugar
- 1 teaspoon Dijon mustard
- 1/2 teaspoon salt
- 1/4 teaspoon black pepper

Directions:

1. Combine in a big bowl the kidney beans, green beans, chickpeas, red onion, red bell pepper, and chopped parsley.
2. Whisk the apple cider vinegar, olive oil, sugar, Dijon mustard, salt, and black pepper until thoroughly blended in a small bowl.
3. Drizzle the dressing over the bean mixture, then toss to coat evenly.
4. To let the tastes marry, cover and chill for at least one hour.
5. Turn the salad gently to distribute the dressing before serving.

Nutritional Information:

Calories: 130, Protein: 4g, Carbohydrates: 18g, Fat: 5g, Fiber: 5g, Cholesterol: 0 mg, Sodium: 300 mg, Potassium: 270 mg

Freekeh And Kale Salad

4 SERVINGS   **15 MINUTES**   **25 MINUTES**

Ingredients:

- 1 cup Freekeh
- 2 cups Water
- 1 bunch Kale, washed, stems removed, and chopped
- 1 can (15 oz) Chickpeas, drained and rinsed
- 1/2 cup Dried Cranberries
- 1/4 cup Sunflower Seeds
- 1 small Red Onion, finely chopped
- 1/4 cup Olive Oil
- 2 tablespoons Lemon Juice
- 1 tablespoon Honey
- 1 clove Garlic, minced
- Salt and Pepper to taste

Directions:

1. Rine one cup freekeh under cold water. Bring two cups of water to a boil in a medium-pot. Add the freekeh, cut heat to low, cover, and simmer for roughly 20 to 25 minutes or until the water is absorbed and the freekeh is soft. Allow it to cool.
2. Get the kale ready: Set the chopped kale in a big salad dish while the freekeh is cooking. Massage the kale for two to three minutes till it softens.
3. Mix ingredients: To the greens add the chickpeas, dried cranberries, sunflower seeds, and red onion.
4. Prepare the dressing. Whisk together in a small bowl olive oil, lemon juice, honey, minced garlic, salt, and pepper.
5. Create the salad by combining: Put the freekeh in the salad dish once it has chilled. Drizzle the dressing over the salad and stir-through.
6. Store refrigerated for up to two days or served straight away.

Nutritional Information:

Calories: 385, Protein: 12g, Carbohydrates: 72g, Fat: 10g, Fiber: 10g, Cholesterol: 0mg, Sodium: 320mg, Potassium: 650mg

Wheatberry And Pomegranate Salad

6 SERVINGS | **15 MINUTES** | **45 MINUTES**

Ingredients:

- 1 cup wheatberries
- 3 cups water
- 1/2 teaspoon salt
- 1 cup pomegranate seeds
- 1/2 cup chopped fresh parsley
- 1/4 cup chopped red onion
- 1/4 cup crumbled feta cheese
- 1/4 cup chopped walnuts
- 3 tablespoons olive oil
- 2 tablespoons balsamic vinegar
- 1 tablespoon honey
- 1/2 teaspoon black pepper

Directions:

1. Before boiling the wheatberries, rine them in cold water. Put together in a large pot wheatberries, water, and salt. Boil; then, lower heat and simmer for 45 minutes or until the wheatberries are tender. Drain then leave to cool.
2. In a small bowl, whisk balsamic vinegar, olive oil, honey, and black pepper until fully combined.
3. Combine Components: Combine in a big mixing bowl cooked wheatberries, pomegranate seeds, parsley, red onion, feta cheese, and walnuts.
4. Drizzle the salad ingredients with the dressing, then gently mix to coat uniformly.
5. Present right away, or chill in the refrigerator for up to one hour to let flavors marry.

Nutritional Information:

Calories: 290, Protein: 7g, Carbohydrates: 39g, Fat: 13g, Fiber: 7g, Cholesterol: 10mg, Sodium: 270mg, Potassium: 340mg

---

Black-Eyed Pea Salad

4 SERVINGS | **15 MINUTES** | **30 MINUTES**

Ingredients:

- 1 cup dried black-eyed peas (or 2 cups canned, rinsed and drained)
- 1/2 cup red bell pepper, diced
- 1/2 cup cucumber, diced
- 1/4 cup red onion, finely chopped
- 1/4 cup fresh parsley, chopped
- 1/4 cup fresh cilantro, chopped
- 1/4 cup extra-virgin olive oil
- 2 tbsp red wine vinegar
- 1 tbsp lemon juice
- 1 garlic clove, minced
- 1 tsp ground cumin
- Salt and pepper to taste

Directions:

1. Cook the black-eyed peas in a pot covered with water if using dry peas. Boil; then, lower to a simmer and cook for around half an hour, or until tender. Drain then let cool. Just rinse and drain canned peas if you're using them.
2. Get the veggies ready: Cube the red bell pepper and cucumber, finely chop the red onion, parsley, and cilantro as the black-eyed peas cool.
3. Create the dressing like this: Whisk together in a small bowl the olive oil, red wine vinegar, lemon juice, minced garlic, ground cumin, salt, and pepper.
4. Add the components: Combine in a big bowl the chilled black-eyed peas, chopped red bell pepper, cucumber, red onion, parsley, and cilantro. Drizzle the dressing over the salad then gently toss to mix.
5. Taste and change seasoning using additional salt and pepper if necessary. To let the flavors mingle, chill the salad in the refrigerator for at least half-hour before presenting.

Nutritional Information:

Calories: 210, Protein: 7g, Carbohydrates: 23g, Fat: 12g, Fiber: 6g, Cholesterol: 0mg, Sodium: 105mg, Potassium: 340mg

Spelt And Roasted Pepper Salad

🍽 4 SERVINGS   ⏱ 15 MINUTES   🕓 45 MINUTES

Ingredients:

- 1 cup spelt (uncooked)
- 2 large red bell peppers
- 1 small red onion, finely chopped
- 1/2 cup cherry tomatoes, halved
- 1/4 cup fresh parsley, chopped
- 2 cups arugula
- 1/4 cup feta cheese, crumbled
- 1/4 cup olive oil
- 2 tablespoons red wine vinegar
- 1 clove garlic, minced
- Salt and pepper to taste

Directions:

1. Rine one cup spelt under cold water. Add the three cups of water and spelt to a medium pot. Boil; then, decrease the heat and let it simmer for forty to forty-five minutes, or until the grains soften. Let cool after draining.
2. Set the oven to 400°F (200°C). On a baking sheet, place two big red bell peppers and roast for 20 to 25 minutes, rotating often until the skin turns roasted. Pull from the oven, let cool, then peel off the skins. Slice peppers into thin strips.
3. Combine the cooled spelt, roasted pepper strips, one finely chopped small red onion, and one half-cup halved cherry tomatoes in a large mixing basin.
4. To the mix add two cups arugula and one-fourth cup chopped fresh parsley. Toss lightly to mix.
5. Whisk one-fourth cup olive oil, two tablespoons red wine vinegar, and one chopped garlic clove in a small bowl. Taste and season with salt and pepper.
6. Drizzle the salad with the dressing; then, toss carefully to coat consistently.
7. On top before serving, sprinkle 1/4 cup crumbled feta cheese.

Nutritional Information:

Calories: 320, Protein: 10g, Carbohydrates: 38g, Fat: 15g, Fiber: 7g, Cholesterol: 12mg, Sodium: 220mg, Potassium: 500mg

Tabbouleh Salad

🍽 6 SERVINGS   ⏱ 20 MINUTES   🕓 10 MINUTES

Ingredients:

- 1 cup bulgur wheat
- 1 1/2 cups boiling water
- 1 medium cucumber, diced
- 2 medium tomatoes, diced
- 1 bunch fresh parsley, finely chopped
- 1/4 cup fresh mint leaves, finely chopped
- 1/4 cup red onion, finely chopped
- 1/4 cup olive oil
- 1/4 cup lemon juice
- 1 tsp salt
- 1/2 tsp black pepper

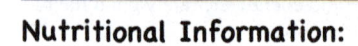

Directions:

1. Arange the bulgur wheat in a big bowl. Pour boiling water over the bulgur, cover, and let sit for 10 minutes until the water absorbs and the bulgur softens.
2. Fluff the bulgur wheat with a fork; let it cool to room temperature.
3. To the bowl containing the cooled bulgur, toss sliced cucumbers, tomatoes, parsley, mint, and red onion.
4. Whisk olive oil, salt, lemon juice and black pepper in a small bowl.
5. Drizzle the dressing over the vegetables and bulgur; toss to completely mix.
6. Before serving, let the salad sit for at least fifteen minutes so the flavors mingle together.
7. Present room temperature or cold.

Nutritional Information:

Calories: 150, Protein: 3g, Carbohydrates: 21g, Fat: 7g, Fiber: 4g, Cholesterol: 0mg, Sodium: 160mg, Potassium: 350mg

Protein-Packed Tofu and Egg Salads

Tofu Caesar Salad

4 SERVINGS 15 MINUTES 10 MINUTES

Ingredients:

- 200g Tofu
- 1 tbsp Olive Oil
- 2 Garlic Cloves, minced
- 1 tbsp Soy Sauce
- 4 cups Romaine Lettuce, chopped
- 1/4 cup Grated Parmesan Cheese
- 1 cup Cherry Tomatoes, halved
- 1/2 cup Croutons
- 1 tbsp Lemon Juice
- 1/2 tsp Dijon Mustard
- Salt and Pepper to taste

Directions:

1. Warm the oven up to 190°C (375°F).
2. To get rid of extra water, press the tofu and then cut it into 1-inch cubes.
3. Tofu cubes, olive oil, chopped garlic, and soy sauce should all be mixed together in a bowl. Toss to cover.
4. On a baking sheet, spread out the tofu. Bake for 10 minutes, or until it turns golden brown. Take it off and let it cool.
5. Chop up romaine lettuce and put it in a big salad bowl. Add grated Parmesan cheese, cherry tomatoes, and croutons.
6. Mix lemon juice, Dijon mustard, and a pinch of salt and pepper in a small bowl with a whisk.
7. Cover the salad with the sauce and add the baked tofu on top of it. Sprinkle to mix.
8. Serve right away.

Nutritional Information:

Calories: 210, Protein: 10g, Carbohydrates: 12g, Fat: 14g, Fiber: 3g, Cholesterol: 2mg, Sodium: 400mg, Potassium: 350mg

Curried Tofu Salad

4 SERVINGS 15 MINUTES 10 MINUTES

Ingredients:

- 1 block (14 oz) extra-firm tofu, drained and pressed
- 1 tablespoon olive oil
- 2 tablespoons curry powder
- 1/4 cup vegan mayonnaise
- 1 tablespoon Dijon mustard
- 1 tablespoon lemon juice
- 1/2 cup red bell pepper, finely diced
- 1/2 cup celery, finely diced
- 1/4 cup red onion, finely diced
- 2 tablespoons fresh cilantro, chopped
- Salt and pepper to taste

Directions:

1. To make the tofu, drain it and press it out. Then, cut it into small cubes. Over medium-low heat, warm the olive oil in a big pan. It will take about 10 minutes of cooking after adding the tofu cubes until they are golden brown and crispy on all sides. Take it off the heat.
2. To make the dressing, mix the curry powder, vegan mayonnaise, Dijon mustard, and lemon juice in a big bowl using a whisk. Make sure the mixture is smooth and well mixed.
3. Mix the ingredients: You can mix the cooked tofu with the red onion, celery, red bell pepper, and parsley in a bowl. Toss everything gently until it's all covered in the sauce.
4. Season: Add salt and pepper to taste to the salad. If needed, change any spices.
5. Serve: You can serve it right away or put it in the fridge to cool down for up to two hours before you serve it.

Nutritional Information:

Calories: 200, Protein: 12g, Carbohydrates: 8g, Fat: 14g, Fiber: 3g, Cholesterol: 0mg, Sodium: 350mg, Potassium: 230mg

Tofu And Mango Salad

4 SERVINGS **15 MINUTES** **0 MINUTES**

Ingredients:

- 14 oz (400g) firm tofu, cubed
- 1 large mango, peeled and diced
- 1 small red bell pepper, diced
- 1 small cucumber, diced
- 2 cups mixed salad greens
- 1/4 cup red onion, finely sliced
- 1/4 cup fresh cilantro leaves, chopped
- 2 tbsp lime juice
- 2 tbsp olive oil
- 1 tbsp soy sauce
- 1 tbsp honey (optional)
- Salt and pepper to taste

Directions:

1. Get the tofu and mango ready. For the tofu, cut it into small cubes. Peel the mango and cut it into cubes of about the same size.
2. Mix the main parts together: Put the diced mango, red bell pepper, cucumber, mixed salad greens, red onion, and fresh cilantro in a big salad bowl.
3. Get the dressing ready: Whisk the olive oil, lime juice, soy sauce, and honey (if using) together in a small bowl until everything is well mixed. Add pepper and salt to taste.
4. Put the salad together: Pour the dressing over the salad ingredients and gently toss to mix. Make sure the dressing covers all the ingredients evenly.
5. Serve fresh: You can serve it right away or put it in the fridge for 10 to 15 minutes to let the tastes blend.

Nutritional Information:

Calories: 220, Protein: 10g, Carbohydrates: 20g, Fat: 12g, Fiber: 4g, Cholesterol: 0mg, Sodium: 340mg, Potassium: 450mg

Grilled Tofu And Vegetable Salad

4 SERVINGS **15 MINUTES** **20 MINUTES**

Ingredients:

- 1 block (14 ounces) extra-firm tofu, pressed and sliced into 1/2 inch thick slices
- 2 tablespoons olive oil
- 1 teaspoon soy sauce
- 1 teaspoon garlic powder
- 1 red bell pepper, sliced into strips
- 1 yellow bell pepper, sliced into strips
- 1 zucchini, sliced into rounds
- 1 small red onion, sliced into rings
- 4 cups mixed salad greens
- 1/4 cup balsamic vinaigrette
- Salt and pepper to taste

Directions:

1. Warm up the grill over medium-high heat.
2. Put 1 tablespoon of olive oil, soy sauce, and garlic powder in a small bowl and mix them together. Spread this on both sides of the tofu pieces with a brush.
3. On the grill, put the red and yellow bell peppers, zucchini, red onion, and tofu pieces. Each side should be cooked for 5 to 7 minutes, or until the veggies are soft and the tofu has grill marks.
4. Take the veggies and tofu off the grill and let them cool down a bit.
5. Cut up the grilled tofu and veggies so that they are easy to eat.
6. Put the mixed salad greens on a plate to serve. The grilled veggies and chopped tofu should be put on top.
7. Put the balsamic dressing on top of the salad, and then add salt and pepper to taste.
8. Serve right away and enjoy!

Nutritional Information:

Calories: 220, Protein: 13g, Carbohydrates: 12g, Fat: 14g, Fiber: 4g, Cholesterol: 0mg, Sodium: 310mg, Potassium: 600mg

Tofu And Avocado Salad

🍲 4 SERVINGS   ⏱ 10 MINUTES   🕐 5 MINUTES

Ingredients:

- 200g Firm Tofu, drained and cubed
- 1 Avocado, diced
- 1 cup Cherry Tomatoes, halved
- 1 Cucumber, diced
- 1/4 Red Onion, thinly sliced
- 2 cups Mixed Greens
- 2 tbsp Olive Oil
- 1 tbsp Lemon Juice
- 1 tbsp Soy Sauce
- 1 tbsp Sesame Seeds
- Salt and Pepper, to taste

Directions:

1. Put a pan that doesn't stick on medium heat and add one tablespoon of olive oil. Add the cubed tofu and cook for about 5 minutes, until it turns golden brown.
2. Put the mixed greens, cherry tomatoes, cucumber, red onion, and avocado in a big bowl.
3. Put the tofu that has been cooked into the bowl.
4. To make the dressing, mix the rest of the olive oil, lemon juice, and soy sauce in a small bowl with a whisk.
5. After you pour the sauce over the salad, top it with salt, pepper, and sesame seeds.
6. Toss gently to mix all the ingredients together well. Serve right away.

Nutritional Information:

Calories: 220, Protein: 9g, Carbohydrates: 12g, Fat: 17g, Fiber: 5g, Cholesterol: 0mg, Sodium: 220mg, Potassium: 600mg

Spicy Tofu And Noodle Salad

🍲 4 SERVINGS   ⏱ 15 MINUTES   🕐 10 MINUTES

Ingredients:

- 200 g Extra-firm Tofu, cubed
- 200 g Rice Noodles
- 1 Medium Carrot, julienned
- 1 Medium Cucumber, julienned
- 1 Red Bell Pepper, thinly sliced
- 2 Green Onions, chopped
- 2 tbsp Soy Sauce
- 1 tbsp Sriracha Sauce
- 1 tbsp Rice Vinegar
- 1 clove Garlic, minced
- 1 tsp Fresh Ginger, grated
- 2 tbsp Sesame Oil
- 1 tbsp Sesame Seeds
- Fresh Cilantro, for garnish

Directions:

1. Follow the directions on the package to cook the rice noodles. Remove the water and set it aside.
2. Set the sesame oil on medium heat in a big pan. It will take about 6 to 8 minutes of cooking after adding the tofu cubes until they are golden brown on all sides.
3. For the dressing, put the soy sauce, sriracha sauce, rice vinegar, garlic, and ginger in a small bowl and mix them together.
4. Tofu, carrot, cucumber, red bell pepper, and green onions should all be put in a big salad bowl.
5. To make sure everything is covered, pour the sauce over the salad and toss it around.
6. Put the sesame seeds on top and then add the fresh parsley on top of that.
7. You can serve it right away or put it in the fridge to make it taste better.

Nutritional Information:

Calories: 300, Protein: 12g, Carbohydrates: 45g, Fat: 10g, Fiber: 3g, Cholesterol: 0 mg, Sodium: 800 mg, Potassium: 400 mg

Tofu And Spinach Salad

4 SERVINGS | **15 MINUTES** | **10 MINUTES**

Ingredients:

- 1 block (14 oz) extra-firm tofu, drained and diced
- 6 cups fresh spinach leaves, washed and dried
- 1 cup cherry tomatoes, halved
- 1/4 cup red onion, thinly sliced
- 1 avocado, pitted and diced
- 1/4 cup sunflower seeds
- 2 tbsp olive oil
- 1 tbsp soy sauce or tamari
- 1 tbsp lemon juice
- 1 garlic clove, minced
- Salt and pepper to taste

Directions:

1. Press the tofu to get rid of extra water, and then cut it into cubes that are easy to eat.
2. In a nonstick pan over medium-low heat, heat 1 tablespoon of olive oil. Add the diced tofu and cook for 7 to 10 minutes, stirring every now and then, until the tofu is golden and crispy. Take it off the heat.
3. Mix the rest of the olive oil, soy sauce or tamari, lemon juice, chopped garlic, salt, and pepper in a small bowl with a whisk while the tofu is cooking.
4. Put the cherry tomatoes, red onion, avocado, sunflower seeds, and fresh spinach leaves in a big salad bowl.
5. Place the cooked tofu in the salad bowl and drizzle with the sauce that you just made.
6. Gently toss to make sure that all the ingredients are well mixed and that the sauce covers everything evenly.
7. Serve right away and enjoy!

Nutritional Information:

Calories: 305, Protein: 14g, Carbohydrates: 12g, Fat: 24g, Fiber: 7g, Cholesterol: 0mg, Sodium: 320mg, Potassium: 980mg

Tofu And Edamame Salad

4 SERVINGS | **15 MINUTES** | **5 MINUTES**

Ingredients:

- 1 cup shelled edamame
- 1 block (14 oz) tofu, extra firm, cubed
- 1 cup cherry tomatoes, halved
- 1/2 cup shredded carrots
- 1/4 cup red onion, finely sliced
- 1/4 cup fresh cilantro, chopped
- 2 cups mixed salad greens
- 1 avocado, diced
- Dressing: 3 tablespoons soy sauce or tamari, 1 tablespoon lime juice, 2 tablespoons rice vinegar, one tablespoon sesame oil, 1 teaspoon honey or agave nectar, 1 teaspoon fresh ginger, grated, Salt and pepper to taste

Directions:

1. Boil the edamame for 5 minutes after you take the shells off. Remove the water and set it aside.
2. Put the tofu cubes, cherry tomatoes cut in half, carrots shreds, red onion slices, cilantro chops, and mixed salad greens in a big bowl.
3. To the salad, add the cooked edamame and the diced avocado.
4. Mix the lime juice, honey (or agave nectar), fresh chopped ginger, salt, and pepper in a small bowl with a whisk. Add the soy sauce (or tamari).
5. Pour the dressing over the salad and gently toss it all together.
6. You can serve it right away or put it in the fridge for 15 minutes to let the flavors mix.

Nutritional Information:

Calories: 250, Protein: 14g, Carbohydrates: 18g, Fat: 15g, Fiber: 7g, Cholesterol: 0mg, Sodium: 520mg, Potassium: 650mg

Classic Egg Salad

🍽 4 SERVINGS   ⏱ 15 MINUTES   🕐 10 MINUTES

Ingredients:

- 8 large eggs
- 1/3 cup mayonnaise
- 1 tbsp Dijon mustard
- 1 stalk celery, finely chopped
- 1/4 cup red onion, finely chopped
- 1 tbsp fresh dill, chopped
- Salt and pepper to taste
- 1 tsp lemon juice (optional)

Directions:

1. Cover the eggs with enough water to leave about an inch of space above them in a pot. Don't pack the eggs down.
2. When it starts to boil, take it off the heat, cover it, and let it sit for 10 minutes.
3. Take the eggs out of the hot water and run cold water over them until they are cool enough to handle. Cut the eggs into big chunks after peeling them.
4. Put the celery, red onion, dill, mayonnaise, Dijon mustard, salt, and pepper in a medium bowl. If you want to add lemon juice, do so now.
5. Add the chopped eggs slowly and mix them in well.
6. Put it in the fridge for at least 30 minutes to let the flavors mix. You can put it in a wrap, on whole-grain bread, or on top of a bed of veggies.

Nutritional Information:

Calories: 230, Protein: 11g, Carbohydrates: 3g, Fat: 19g, Fiber: 0g, Cholesterol: 375mg, Sodium: 290mg, Potassium: 140mg

Deviled Egg Salad

🍽 4 SERVINGS   ⏱ 15 MINUTES   🕐 10 MINUTES

Ingredients:

- 8 large eggs
- 1/4 cup mayonnaise
- 1 tbsp Dijon mustard
- 1 tbsp white vinegar
- 1/4 tsp paprika
- Salt and pepper, to taste
- 1/2 cup chopped celery
- 1/4 cup chopped green onions
- 1 tbsp fresh dill, chopped (optional)

Directions:

1. Cover the eggs with water in a pot. Heat it up and bring it to a full boil. Cover the pan and take it off the heat once it starts to boil. Cover the eggs and leave them alone for 10 minutes.
2. Take the eggs out of the hot water and run cold water over them until they feel cool. Peel the eggs and cut them up into small pieces.
3. Put the chopped eggs, mayonnaise, Dijon mustard, white vinegar, paprika, salt, and pepper in a big bowl. Make sure to mix the items well until they are all mixed in.
4. Add the green onions and chopped celery. If you want to add more taste, you can add fresh dill.
5. You can serve the chilled egg salad by itself or on top of a bed of fresh veggies.

Nutritional Information:

Calories: 210, Protein: 10g, Carbohydrates: 3g, Fat: 18g, Fiber: 0g, Cholesterol: 320mg, Sodium: 310mg, Potassium: 140mg

Egg And Bacon Salad

4 SERVINGS   **15 MINUTES**   **10 MINUTES**

Ingredients:

- 4 large eggs
- 6 slices bacon
- 4 cups mixed greens
- 1 cup cherry tomatoes, halved
- 1/2 cup red onion, thinly sliced
- 1 avocado, diced
- 1/4 cup feta cheese, crumbled
- 1/4 cup olive oil
- 2 tbsp balsamic vinegar
- Salt and pepper to taste

Directions:

1. To boil the eggs, put them in a pot and add enough water to cover them. Bring to a boil, then lower the heat and let it cook for 10 minutes. Take the eggs out and run cold water over them to cool them down. Cut the eggs into quarters after peeling them.
2. Heat up a pan over medium-low heat and add the bacon. Cook the bacon for about 6 to 7 minutes, until it turns crispy. Get the bacon out and put it on paper towels to dry. When the bacon is cool, break it up.
3. Put the salad together: Put the mixed leaves, cherry tomatoes cut in half, and red onion slices in a large bowl. Put in the feta cheese and avocado chunks.
4. To dress the salad, mix the olive oil and balsamic vinegar in a small bowl using a whisk. Add pepper and salt.
5. Put in the protein: Put the bacon bits and quartered eggs on top of the salad. Pour the dressing over the salad and gently toss to mix.
6. Serve right away and enjoy!

Nutritional Information:

Calories: 350, Protein: 14g, Carbohydrates: 9g, Fat: 30g, Fiber: 4g, Cholesterol: 220mg, Sodium: 550mg, Potassium: 500mg

Egg And Potato Salad

4 SERVINGS   **20 MINUTES**   **15 MINUTES**

Ingredients:

- 4 large eggs
- 3 medium potatoes, peeled and cubed
- 1/4 cup mayonnaise
- 1/4 cup Greek yogurt
- 2 tablespoons Dijon mustard
- 1/4 cup finely diced red onion
- 1/4 cup finely chopped celery
- 1 tablespoon chopped fresh parsley
- 1 teaspoon salt
- 1/2 teaspoon black pepper
- 1 tablespoon apple cider vinegar

Directions:

1. Cover the eggs with water in a medium-sized pot. Bring to a boil over a medium-high level of heat. Turn off the heat, cover the pan, and let it sit for 12 minutes. Drain the food and put it in a bowl of ice water. When the eggs are cool, peel them and cut them up.
2. Put the cubed potatoes in a big pot and cover them with water. Bring to a boil over medium-high heat. Cook for 10 to 12 minutes, or until the vegetables are soft. Let it cool down after draining.
3. Put the Dijon mustard, mayonnaise, Greek yogurt, red onion, celery, parsley, salt, black pepper, and apple cider vinegar in a big bowl. Mix well.
4. Add the cooled potatoes and chopped eggs to the bowl. Gently fold the ingredients together until they are well mixed and covered in the sauce.
5. You can add more salt and pepper to taste, if necessary.
6. To let the tastes blend, cover and put in the fridge for at least 30 minutes before serving.

Nutritional Information:

Calories: 240, Protein: 8g, Carbohydrates: 21g, Fat: 15g, Fiber: 3g, Cholesterol: 210 mg, Sodium: 520 mg, Potassium: 620 mg

Egg And Avocado Salad

🍽 4 SERVINGS ⏱ 10 MINUTES 🕙 10 MINUTES

Ingredients:

- 4 large eggs
- 2 ripe avocados, diced
- 1/4 cup red onion, finely chopped
- 2 tablespoons fresh cilantro, chopped
- 2 tablespoons lime juice
- 1 tablespoon olive oil
- 1/2 teaspoon salt
- 1/4 teaspoon black pepper
- 1/4 teaspoon garlic powder

Directions:

1. Put the eggs in a pot and add water to cover them. Bring to a boil over a medium-high level of heat. Turn down the heat to low and let it cook for 10 minutes after it starts to boil.
2. Prepare the other ingredients while the eggs are cooking. Cut the red onion and parsley into small pieces, and dice the avocados.
3. Put the eggs in a bowl of ice water to cool down after they're done. Cut the eggs into small pieces that are easy to eat.
4. Put the diced avocados, red onion, cilantro, and chopped eggs in a big bowl.
5. Mix the olive oil, salt, lime juice, garlic powder and black pepper in a small bowl with a whisk.
6. Add the sauce to the egg and avocado mix. Toss the ingredients gently to coat them all.
7. You can serve it right away or put it in the fridge for up to two hours to let the flavors mix.

Nutritional Information:

Calories: 220, Protein: 7g, Carbohydrates: 6g, Fat: 18g, Fiber: 6g, Cholesterol: 187mg, Sodium: 300mg, Potassium: 485mg

Egg And Tomato Salad

🍽 4 SERVINGS ⏱ 10 MINUTES 🕙 10 MINUTES

Ingredients:

- 4 large eggs
- 2 cups cherry tomatoes, halved
- 1/4 cup red onion, finely chopped
- 1/4 cup fresh basil, chopped
- 2 tablespoons olive oil
- 1 tablespoon balsamic vinegar
- Salt and pepper to taste

Directions:

1. Cover the eggs with cold water and put them in a pot.
2. Over medium-high heat, bring the water to a boil.
3. Take the pot off the heat when the water starts to boil very quickly. Cover it and leave it alone for 10 minutes.
4. Get the other things ready while the eggs are cooking. Cut the cherry tomatoes in half and the red onion and basil into small pieces.
5. Set the eggs in a bowl of ice water for 10 minutes. This will stop the cooking process and cool them down.
6. After the eggs have cooled, peel them and cut them up into small pieces.
7. Put the chopped eggs, cherry tomatoes, red onion, and basil in a big bowl.
8. Mix the olive oil, salt, balsamic vinegar, and pepper in a small bowl with a whisk.
9. Add the dressing to the salad and mix it together gently.
10. Serve right away or put in the fridge until you're ready to serve.

Nutritional Information:

Calories: 170, Protein: 8g, Carbohydrates: 5g, Fat: 13g, Fiber: 1g, Cholesterol: 187mg, Sodium: 150mg, Potassium: 250mg

Egg And Cucumber Salad

4 SERVINGS **15 MINUTES** **10 MINUTES**

Ingredients:

- 4 large eggs
- 1 medium cucumber, diced
- 1/4 cup red onion, finely chopped
- 1/4 cup plain Greek yogurt
- 1 tablespoon Dijon mustard
- 1 tablespoon fresh dill, chopped
- 1 tablespoon lemon juice
- Salt and pepper to taste
- Mixed greens for serving

Directions:

1. Cover the eggs with cold water and put them in a pot. Heat it up and bring it to a boil.
2. Turn down the heat to low and let the eggs cook for 10 minutes.
3. Take the eggs out of the pot and quickly put them in a bowl of ice water to cool down.
4. After the eggs have cooled, peel them and cut them in half.
5. Put the diced cucumber, chopped red onion, Greek yogurt, Dijon mustard, fresh dill, and lemon juice in a big bowl.
6. Add the quartered eggs slowly, mixing them in until they are well covered.
7. Add salt and pepper to the salad as needed.
8. Put the egg and cucumber salad on top of a bed of mixed greens.

Nutritional Information:

Calories: 150, Protein: 12g, Carbohydrates: 5g, Fat: 7g, Fiber: 1g, Cholesterol: 190mg, Sodium: 220mg, Potassium: 200mg

Mediterranean Egg Salad

4 SERVINGS **15 MINUTES** **10 MINUTES**

Ingredients:

- 6 large eggs
- 1 cup cherry tomatoes, halved
- 1/2 cup cucumber, diced
- 1/4 cup red onion, finely chopped
- 1/4 cup Kalamata olives, pitted and sliced
- 1/4 cup feta cheese, crumbled
- 2 tablespoons fresh parsley, chopped
- 2 tablespoons extra-virgin olive oil
- 1 tablespoon red wine vinegar
- 1 teaspoon Dijon mustard
- Salt and pepper, to taste

Directions:

1. Put the eggs in a pot and add enough water to cover them. Bring to a boil over a medium-high level of heat. Once it starts to boil, turn down the heat and let it cook for 9 to 10 minutes.
2. Prepare the salad while the eggs are cooking. Cut the cherry tomatoes in half, dice the cucumber, finely chop the red onion, slice the Kalamata olives, crumble the feta cheese, and chop the fresh herbs.
3. After the eggs are done, drain them and put them in a bowl of ice water for five minutes to cool down. Cut the eggs into small pieces that you can easily eat.
4. Put the chopped eggs, cherry tomatoes, cucumber, red onion, feta cheese, olives and parsley in a big bowl.
5. Add the olive oil, red wine vinegar, Dijon mustard, salt, and pepper to a small bowl. Use a whisk to mix the ingredients well.
6. Spread the dressing out on the salad and gently toss it to cover everything.
7. Serve right away or put in the fridge to enjoy later.

Nutritional Information:

Calories: 220, Protein: 10g, Carbohydrates: 6g, Fat: 18g, Fiber: 1.5g, Cholesterol: 210mg, Sodium: 390mg, Potassium: 220mg

Light and Fresh Seafood Salads

Classic Tuna Salad

🍽 4 SERVINGS ⏱ 15 MINUTES 🕐 0 MINUTES

Ingredients:

- 2 cans (5 oz each) tuna packed in water, drained
- 1/4 cup mayonnaise
- 2 tablespoons Dijon mustard
- 1 stalk celery, finely chopped
- 1/4 cup red onion, finely chopped
- 1 tablespoon fresh lemon juice
- 2 tablespoons relish (optional)
- Salt and pepper to taste
- Mixed salad greens for serving
- Optional garnishes: cherry tomatoes, cucumber slices, hard-boiled eggs

Directions:

1. Combine the Dijon mustard, mayonnaise and drained tuna in a big bowl. Stir thoroughly until the tuna is evenly covered.
2. To the tuna mix add the chopped celery and red onion. Stirring till blended will help.
3. Add the fresh lemon juice and, if using, relish. Mix until every component is uniformly distributed.
4. Taste and season according on need using salt and pepper.
5. Present the tuna salad on a bed of mixed salad greens and top if preferred with hard-boiled eggs, cucumber slices, or cherry tomatoes.

Nutritional Information:

Calories: 180, Protein: 18g, Carbohydrates: 3g, Fat: 10g, Fiber: 1g, Cholesterol: 35mg, Sodium: 430mg, Potassium: 300mg

Shrimp And Avocado Salad

🍽 4 SERVINGS ⏱ 15 MINUTES 🕐 5 MINUTES

Ingredients:

- 1 lb (450g) shrimp, peeled and deveined
- 2 medium avocados, diced
- 1 cup cherry tomatoes, halved
- 1/2 red onion, thinly sliced
- 1/4 cup fresh cilantro, chopped
- 1 lime, juiced
- 2 tbsp olive oil
- 1 tsp salt
- 1/2 tsp black pepper
- 1/4 tsp red pepper flakes (optional)
- 4 cups mixed greens

Directions:

1. Bring a big saucepan of water to a boil and sprinkle some salt. Add the shrimp and cook, roughly three to four minutes, until they turn pink and opaque. Sort and let cool.
2. Combine in a large bowl the chopped avocados, cherry tomatoes, red onion, and cilantro.
3. Whisk the lime juice, olive oil, salt, black pepper, and red pepper flakes if using in a small bowl.
4. Add the chilled prawns to the avocado mixture; then, top with dressing. Toss gently to mix.
5. Top a bed of mixed greens with the prawn and avocado mixture.

Nutritional Information:

Calories: 310, Protein: 22g, Carbohydrates: 12g, Fat: 22g, Fiber: 8g, Cholesterol: 200mg, Sodium: 680mg, Potassium: 980mg

Crab And Corn Salad

4 SERVINGS | **15 MINUTES** | **0 MINUTES**

Ingredients:

- 1 lb (450g) fresh crab meat, picked over for shells
- 1 cup (160g) cooked corn kernels (fresh or frozen)
- 1/2 cup (80g) diced red bell pepper
- 1/4 cup (40g) finely chopped red onion
- 1/4 cup (40g) sliced green onions
- 1/4 cup (60ml) mayonnaise
- 2 tbsp (30ml) fresh lime juice
- 1 tbsp (15ml) olive oil
- 1 tbsp (15g) chopped fresh cilantro
- Salt, to taste
- Freshly ground black pepper, to taste
- Mixed salad greens, for serving (optional)

Directions:

1. Combine in a big bowl the crab meat, red bell pepper, corn kernels, red onion, and green onions.
2. Whisk together in a small bowl the olive oil, lime juice, mayonnaise, and chopped cilantro until thoroughly blended.
3. Drizzle the dressing over the crab mixture then gently toss to blend.
4. Taste and generously sprinkle fresh ground black pepper and salt.
5. If preferred, place the crab and corn salad on a bed of mixed salad greens for a fresh and vibrant display.

Nutritional Information:

Calories: 240, Protein: 21g, Carbohydrates: 14g, Fat: 12g, Fiber: 2g, Cholesterol: 80mg, Sodium: 600mg, Potassium: 420mg

Salmon And Dill Salad

4 SERVINGS | **15 MINUTES** | **10 MINUTES**

Ingredients:

- 2 large salmon fillets (about 6 oz each)
- Salt and pepper to taste
- 1 tablespoon olive oil
- 1 cup diced cucumber
- 1 cup halved cherry tomatoes
- 1/4 cup thinly sliced red onion
- 2 tablespoons fresh dill, chopped
- 2 tablespoons capers, drained
- 3 cups mixed greens
- 1 lemon, juiced
- 1 tablespoon Dijon mustard
- 3 tablespoons extra-virgin olive oil

Directions:

1. Turn a grill or skillet's temperature medium-high. Sprink the salmon fillets with salt and pepper.
2. Drizzle on the grill or skillet one tablespoon of olive oil. Salmon should be cooked through and flake readily with a fork after about 4 to 5 minutes on each side. Take off of the burner and let cool.
3. Combine in a large bowl the sliced red onion, chopped dill, halved cherry tomatoes, diced cucumber, and drained capers.
4. Whisk together in a small bowl the extra-virgin olive oil, Dijon mustard, and lemon juice. Taste then add salt and pepper.
5. After flaking the cooled salmon into bite-sized bits, toss them into the big bowl with the vegetables. Add the mixed greens now.
6. Drizzle the salad with the dressing then gently toss to mix.
7. To let the flavors mingle, serve straight away or chill for up to two hours before.

Nutritional Information:

Calories: 290, Protein: 22g, Carbohydrates: 7g, Fat: 19g, Fiber: 2g, Cholesterol: 55 mg, Sodium: 230 mg, Potassium: 600 mg

Smoked Salmon And Cucumber Salad

🍽 4 SERVINGS　⏱ 15 MINUTES　🕐 0 MINUTES

Ingredients:

- 8 oz smoked salmon, thinly sliced
- 2 large cucumbers, thinly sliced
- 1 small red onion, thinly sliced
- 1/4 cup fresh dill, chopped
- 1/4 cup capers, drained
- 1 lemon, juiced
- 2 tbsp olive oil
- Salt and pepper to taste

Directions:

1. On a platter or in a big salad bowl, equally arrange the sliced cucumbers.
2. Lay the thinly sliced smoked salmon over the cucumbers.
3. Over the salad evenly sprinkle fresh dill, capers, and thinly sliced red onion.
4. To make the dressing, whisk together in a small bowl the lemon juice, olive oil, salt, and pepper.
5. Over the salad, evenly drizzle the dressing.
6. To mix all the ingredients and guarantee proper dressing distribution, toss lightly.
7. Either chill until ready to eat or serve straight away.

Nutritional Information:

Calories: 200, Protein: 15g, Carbohydrates: 8g, Fat: 12g, Fiber: 2g, Cholesterol: 25 mg, Sodium: 800 mg, Potassium: 600 mg

Scallop And Mango Salad

🍽 4 SERVINGS　⏱ 15 MINUTES　🕐 10 MINUTES

Ingredients:

- 1 lb fresh scallops
- 1 large mango, diced
- 1 medium red bell pepper, diced
- 1 small red onion, finely chopped
- 1 cup cherry tomatoes, halved
- ½ cup fresh cilantro leaves, chopped
- 2 tbsp olive oil
- 2 tbsp lime juice
- 1 tbsp honey
- Salt and pepper to taste
- 4 cups mixed greens

Directions:

1. Under cold water, rinse the scallops; then, use paper towels to pat dry. Season using salt and pepper.
2. In a large skillet set on medium-high, heat one tablespoon of olive oil. Add the scallops and cook, on each side, 2 to 4 minutes, or until gently browned and cooked through. Take off from the heat and set aside.
3. Combine in a big bowl the diced mango, red onion, cherry tomatoes, red bell pepper, and cilantro.
4. Whisk remaining olive oil, lime juice, honey, salt, and pepper in a small bowl.
5. Add the seared scallops to the salad mixture and gently toss with the dressing until thoroughly blended.
6. On every plate, set a bed of mixed greens and top with the scallop and mango concoction.
7. Present right away and have fun.

Nutritional Information:

Calories: 240, Protein: 20g, Carbohydrates: 18g, Fat: 11g, Fiber: 3g, Cholesterol: 35 mg, Sodium: 320 mg, Potassium: 550 mg

Seafood Pasta Salad

🍽️ 4 SERVINGS ⏱️ 15 MINUTES 🕐 10 MINUTES

Ingredients:

- 8 oz cooked pasta (such as rotini or penne)
- 1/2 lb cooked shrimp, peeled and deveined
- 1/2 lb cooked crab meat
- 1 cup cherry tomatoes, halved
- 1/2 cup red bell pepper, diced
- 1/2 cup cucumber, diced
- 1/4 cup red onion, thinly sliced
- 1/4 cup black olives, sliced
- 1/4 cup fresh parsley, chopped
- 1/4 cup lemon juice
- 1/4 cup olive oil
- 1 tsp Dijon mustard
- 1 garlic clove, minced
- Salt and pepper to taste

Directions:

1. Follow package directions for cooking the pasta. To cool, drain and rinse beneath cold water.
2. Combine in a big bowl the cooked pasta, prawns, crab meat, cherry tomatoes, red bell pepper, cucumber, red onion, black olives, and parsley.
3. To create the dressing, toss in a small bowl the lemon juice, olive oil, Dijon mustard, minced garlic, salt, and pepper.
4. Drizzle the dressing over the pasta salad then toss to evenly coat everything.
5. To let the tastes marry, chill the salad for at least half an hour before serving.
6. Present cold and savorable.

Nutritional Information:

Calories: 340, Protein: 20g, Carbohydrates: 30g, Fat: 15g, Fiber: 3g, Cholesterol: 120 mg, Sodium: 600 mg, Potassium: 450 mg

Lobster And Asparagus Salad

🍽️ 4 SERVINGS ⏱️ 15 MINUTES 🕐 10 MINUTES

Ingredients:

- 2 lbs fresh lobster tails
- 1 lb asparagus, trimmed and cut into 2-inch pieces
- 2 cups mixed greens (arugula, spinach, and watercress)
- 1 cup cherry tomatoes, halved
- 1 avocado, sliced
- 1 lemon, juiced
- 2 tbsp olive oil
- 1 tbsp fresh dill, chopped
- Salt and pepper to taste

Directions:

1. Bring a big salted water pot to boil. Add the lobster tails and simmer for eight to ten minutes, or until the meat is opaque and the shells are brilliant red. Cut off the lobster tails and let them cool just little.
2. Blanch the asparagus bits for two to three minutes in the same saucepan until tender-crisp. To halt the cooking, drain and submerge them into an ice bath. Drain once more and reserve.
3. Remove the meat from the shells after the lobster is cool enough to handle, then chop into bite-sized bits.
4. Combine in a large salad bowl the mixed greens, cherry tomatoes, avocado, blanched asparagus.
5. Top with the lobster meat.
6. Whisk together in a small bowl the lemon juice, olive oil, minced dill, salt, and pepper.
7. Drizzle the salad with the dressing; then, gently toss to mix.
8. Eat right away.

Nutritional Information:

Calories: 320, Protein: 28g, Carbohydrates: 8g, Fat: 20g, Fiber: 5g, Cholesterol: 145 mg, Sodium: 460 mg, Potassium: 850 mg

Calamari And Tomato Salad

4 SERVINGS   **15 MINUTES**   **10 MINUTES**

Ingredients:

- 1 lb (450 g) fresh calamari, cleaned and sliced into rings
- 2 cups cherry tomatoes, halved
- 1 small red onion, thinly sliced
- 1/4 cup fresh basil leaves, chopped
- 2 tbsp extra virgin olive oil
- 1 tbsp lemon juice
- 1 clove garlic, minced
- Salt and black pepper to taste
- Optional: red pepper flakes for a bit of heat

Directions:

1. Bring a big salted water pot to boiling point.
2. Add the calamari rings and heat until opaque and tender, two to three minutes. Try not to overcook them.
3. To halt cooking, drain the calamari and rinse under cool water.
4. Combine the red onion, fresh basil, cooked calamari, cherry tomatoes in a big bowl.
5. Whisk olive oil, lemon juice, minced garlic, salt, black pepper—and red pepper flakes if using—in a small bowl.
6. Drizzle the dressing over tomato mixture and calamari, then gently toss to cover.
7. To let the flavors marry, let the salad sit for roughly five minutes.
8. Store refrigerated until up to two hours before serving or straight away.

Nutritional Information:

Calories: 180, Protein: 20g, Carbohydrates: 6g, Fat: 10g, Fiber: 2g, Cholesterol: 200 mg, Sodium: 280 mg, Potassium: 450 mg

Prawn And Watermelon Salad

4 SERVINGS   **15 MINUTES**   **5 MINUTES**

Ingredients:

- 1 lb (450g) peeled and deveined prawns
- 2 cups diced watermelon
- 1 small red onion, thinly sliced
- 1 avocado, diced
- 1 cup arugula
- 1/4 cup fresh mint leaves, roughly chopped
- 1/4 cup fresh lime juice
- 2 tbsp olive oil
- 1 tbsp honey
- Salt and pepper to taste

Directions:

1. Set a non-stick skillet over medium-high heat. Add the prawns; cook on each side for two to three minutes until opaque and pink. Take off from the heat and let cool.
2. Combine in a big mixing dish the chopped watermelon, red onion, avocado, arugula, and mint leaves.
3. To make the dressing, whisk together in a small bowl the lime juice, olive oil, honey, salt, and pepper.
4. Add the cooked prawns to the salad mixture and gently stir.
5. Drizzle the dressing over the salad; then, toss one more to guarantee equal coating.
6. Deliver right away.

Nutritional Information:

Calories: 220, Protein: 20g, Carbohydrates: 18g, Fat: 10g, Fiber: 4g, Cholesterol: 150mg, Sodium: 220mg, Potassium: 650mg

Sardine And Potato Salad

 4 SERVINGS   15 MINUTES   20 MINUTES

Ingredients:

- 4 large potatoes, peeled and cut into 1-inch cubes
- 1 can (4.375 oz) sardines in olive oil, drained and flaked
- 1 small red onion, thinly sliced
- 1/4 cup chopped fresh parsley
- 1/4 cup extra-virgin olive oil
- 2 tablespoons freshly squeezed lemon juice
- 1 tablespoon Dijon mustard
- Salt and pepper, to taste
- 1 cup mixed salad greens

Directions:

1. Bring a big salted water pot to boil over high heat. Add the potato cubes and simmer, for fifteen minutes, until cooked. Drain and let to chill somewhat.
2. Combine sliced red onion, minced parsley, and flaked sardines in a big mixing basin.
3. Whisk olive oil, lemon juice, and Dijon mustard until well blended in a small bowl. Taste-test and season with salt and pepper.
4. Add the cooked potatoes to the sardine mixture and softly stir to blend.
5. Drizzle the dressing over the salad then gently mix to evenly coat every component.
6. Arrange four dishes with the mixed salad greens, then top with the sardine and potato combination.
7. Present right away; sprinkle extra parsley, if preferred.

Nutritional Information:

Calories: 290, Protein: 10g, Carbohydrates: 26g, Fat: 17g, Fiber: 3g, Cholesterol: 40mg, Sodium: 220mg, Potassium: 700mg

Octopus And Olive Salad

 4 SERVINGS   20 MINUTES   30 MINUTES

Ingredients:

- 1 lb octopus, cleaned and prepared
- 1/2 cup pitted green olives, halved
- 1/2 cup pitted black olives, halved
- 1 cup cherry tomatoes, halved
- 1 small red onion, thinly sliced
- 2 tbsp fresh parsley, chopped
- 1/4 cup extra-virgin olive oil
- 2 tbsp red wine vinegar
- Juice of 1 lemon
- 1 tsp dried oregano
- Salt and pepper to taste
- 1 clove garlic, minced

Directions:

1. Pour a lot of water into a big saucepan and bring it boiling. Load the boiling water with the cleaned and ready octopus. Lower the heat and simmer until the octopus is soft, about thirty minutes. Taking the octopus out of the pot, let it cool.
2. Cut the octopus into bite-sized bits once cold and arrange them in a big salad dish.
3. To the bowl containing the octopus add the green and black olives, cherry tomatoes, red onion, parsley.
4. In a small bowl olive oil, red wine vinegar, lemon juice, oregano, minced garlic, salt, and pepper, whisk everything together.
5. Make sure every part is adequately covered; drizzle the dressing over the salad and toss to mix.
6. Before serving, let the salad sit for at least ten minutes so the flavors mingle together.

Nutritional Information:

Calories: 280, Protein: 25g, Carbohydrates: 7g, Fat: 16g, Fiber: 2g, Cholesterol: 80mg, Sodium: 900mg, Potassium: 450mg

Mackerel And Beet Salad

4 SERVINGS   **20 MINUTES**   **40 MINUTES**

Ingredients:

- 2 medium-sized beets
- 2 fillets of smoked mackerel
- 1 cup arugula
- 1 small red onion, thinly sliced
- 1/4 cup crumbled goat cheese
- 2 tablespoons olive oil
- 1 tablespoon balsamic vinegar
- 1 teaspoon Dijon mustard
- Salt and pepper to taste
- 1 tablespoon chopped fresh dill

Directions:

1. Set your oven for 400°F (200°C). After careful washing the beets, wrap each one separately in aluminum foil. Arrange on a baking sheet and roast until soft when fork tested around 40 minutes. Let cool; then cut into cubes after peeling.
2. Prepare the dressing as the beets roast. Whisk together in a small bowl olive oil, Dijon mustard, salt, balsamic vinegar, and pepper until well blended.
3. Remove any bones as you flake the smoked mackerel into bite-sized bits.
4. Combine in a big salad dish the roasted beet cubes, arugula, sliced red onion, flaked mackerel, and crumbled goat cheese.
5. Drizzle the salad with the dressing; gently toss to cover everything evenly.
6. On top as a garnish, scatter the chopped fresh dill.

Nutritional Information:

Calories: 250, Protein: 17g, Carbohydrates: 12g, Fat: 15g, Fiber: 3g, Cholesterol: 45 mg, Sodium: 480 mg, Potassium: 570 mg

Tuna Niçoise Salad

4 SERVINGS   **20 MINUTES**   **10 MINUTES**

Ingredients:

- 2 cans (5 oz each) tuna in olive oil, drained
- 4 cups mixed salad greens
- 2 cups cherry tomatoes, halved
- 1 cup green beans, blanched and trimmed
- 4 hard-boiled eggs, quartered
- 1/2 cup black olives, pitted
- 1 small red onion, thinly sliced
- 4 small new potatoes, boiled and quartered
- 2 tbsp capers
- 2 tbsp fresh parsley, chopped
- 1/4 cup extra-virgin olive oil
- 2 tbsp red wine vinegar
- 1 tbsp Dijon mustard
- Salt and pepper to taste

Directions:

1. Combine in a big bowl mixed salad greens, cherry tomatoes, green beans, red onion, black olives, and capers.
2. Arrange the hard-boiled eggs and boiled, quartered fresh potatoes around the salad mix.
3. After carefully flaking the tuna with a fork, top the salad with it.
4. Whisk together in a small bowl the extra-virgin olive oil, red wine vinegar, Dijon mustard, a little salt and pepper until well blended.
5. Drizzle the salad's dressing uniformly all around.
6. As a garnish, scatter chopped fresh parsley over the salad.
7. Just before serving, toss carefully to mix all the components.

Nutritional Information:

Calories: 420, Protein: 26g, Carbohydrates: 18g, Fat: 28g, Fiber: 4g, Cholesterol: 210mg, Sodium: 520mg, Potassium: 980mg

Grilled Shrimp Caesar Salad

🍽️ 4 SERVINGS   ⏱️ 15 MINUTES   🕐 10 MINUTES

Ingredients:

- 1 lb large shrimp, peeled and deveined
- 2 tbsp olive oil
- 1 tsp garlic powder
- 1 tsp paprika
- 1/4 tsp salt
- 1/4 tsp black pepper
- 1 head romaine lettuce, chopped
- 1/2 cup Caesar dressing
- 1/4 cup grated Parmesan cheese
- 1 cup croutons
- 1 lemon, cut into wedges

Directions:

1. Preheat the grill to medium-high heat.
2. In a bowl, combine shrimp, olive oil, garlic powder, paprika, salt, and black pepper. Toss to coat.
3. Thread shrimp onto skewers, about 4-5 shrimp per skewer.
4. Grill shrimp for 2-4 minutes on each side, until pink and opaque.
5. Combine cut romaine lettuce and Caesar dressing in a big salad bowl. Toss carefully to cover.
6. Add grilled shrimp on top of the dressed lettuce.
7. Sprinkle grated Parmesan cheese and croutons over the salad.
8. Present straight ahead with lemon wedges on the side.

Nutritional Information:

Calories: 420, Protein: 30g, Carbohydrates: 12g, Fat: 29g, Fiber: 2g, Cholesterol: 220mg, Sodium: 900mg, Potassium: 420mg

Spicy Crab Salad

🍽️ 4 SERVINGS   ⏱️ 15 MINUTES   🕐 0 MINUTES

Ingredients:

- 1 lb fresh crab meat, picked over for shells
- 1 cup cucumber, diced
- 1/2 cup radishes, thinly sliced
- 1/4 cup red bell pepper, finely chopped
- 1/4 cup green onion, thinly sliced
- 1 avocado, diced
- 2 tbsp fresh cilantro, chopped
- 1 jalapeño, seeded and minced
- 1/4 cup lime juice (about 2 limes)
- 2 tbsp olive oil
- 1 tbsp hot sauce (adjust to taste)
- Salt and pepper to taste
- Mixed greens or lettuce leaves for serving

Directions:

1. Combine in a big mixing bowl the crab meat, cucumbers, radishes, red bell pepper, green onion, avocado, fresh cilantro, and jalapeño.
2. Whisk together in a small bowl the lime juice, olive oil, and spicy sauce until thoroughly blended.
3. Drizzle the dressing over the crab mixture, then gently toss to coat evenly.
4. Taste should guide the season with salt and pepper.
5. Present the crab salad atop mixed greens or lettuce leaves.

Nutritional Information:

Calories: 220, Protein: 20g, Carbohydrates: 10g, Fat: 12g, Fiber: 4g, Cholesterol: 70mg, Sodium: 450mg, Potassium: 580mg

Flavorful Chicken Salads

Classic Chicken Caesar Salad

4 SERVINGS   20 MINUTES   10 MINUTES

Ingredients:

- 2 cups Romaine lettuce, chopped
- 2 cups cooked chicken breast, sliced
- 1/2 cup Caesar dressing
- 1/4 cup grated Parmesan cheese
- 1 cup croutons
- 1/4 teaspoon black pepper
- 1 clove garlic, minced
- 1 teaspoon lemon juice
- 1 tablespoon olive oil
- 1/2 cup cherry tomatoes, halved (optional)

Directions:

1. Combine Romaine lettuce and sliced chicken breast in a big salad bowl.
2. Combine the Caesar dressing, minced garlic, lemon juice, olive oil until thoroughly blended in a small bowl.
3. Pour the dressing mixture over the lettuce and chicken, then toss well to coat evenly.
4. Sprinkle grated Parmesan cheese and black pepper over the salad.
5. Add croutons and gently toss the salad again.
6. (Optional) Add cherry tomatoes for an extra burst of flavor.
7. Serve the Classic Chicken Caesar Salad immediately.

Nutritional Information:

Calories: 350, Protein: 25g, Carbohydrates: 15g, Fat: 20g, Fiber: 2g, Cholesterol: 70mg, Sodium: 780mg, Potassium: 500mg

Bbq Chicken Salad

4 SERVINGS   15 MINUTES   10 MINUTES

Ingredients:

- 2 cups cooked, shredded chicken breast
- 1/2 cup BBQ sauce
- 4 cups chopped romaine lettuce
- 1 cup cherry tomatoes, halved
- 1/2 cup canned corn, drained and rinsed
- 1/2 cup black beans, drained and rinsed
- 1/4 cup red onion, finely chopped
- 1/2 cup shredded cheddar cheese
- 1 avocado, diced
- 1/4 cup ranch dressing (optional)
- Salt and pepper to taste

Directions:

1. Combine the shredded chicken breast with BBQ sauce till uniformly coated in a large mixing dish.
2. Set the chopped romaine lettuce on a big platter or split it up among many dishes.
3. Evenly distribute the BBQ chicken over the romaine lettuce.
4. Top the salad with cherry tomatoes, canned corn, black beans, and red onion.
5. Sprinkle shredded cheddar cheese over the top.
6. Add the diced avocado.
7. Drizzle with ranch dressing if using, and season with salt and pepper to taste.
8. Toss the salad lightly to combine all ingredients before serving.

Nutritional Information:

Calories: 350, Protein: 30g, Carbohydrates: 25g, Fat: 15g, Fiber: 7g, Cholesterol: 75mg, Sodium: 850mg, Potassium: 800mg

Asian Chicken Salad

4 SERVINGS **20 MINUTES** **15 MINUTES**

Ingredients:

- 2 boneless, skinless chicken breasts
- 1 tablespoon olive oil
- 4 cups mixed greens (spinach, arugula, romaine)
- 1 cup shredded carrots
- 1 cup red cabbage, thinly sliced
- 1 cup edamame, shelled and cooked
- 1 red bell pepper, thinly sliced
- 2 green onions, chopped
- 1/4 cup chopped cilantro
- 1/4 cup sliced almonds
- 1 tablespoon sesame seeds
- For the Dressing: 2 tablespoons rice vinegar, 1 tablespoon sesame oil, 3 tablespoons soy sauce, 1 teaspoon ginger, 2 tablespoons honey, minced, 1 garlic clove, minced, 1 teaspoon sriracha (optional)

Directions:

1. Turn the grill or a grill pan over medium-high heat. Olive oil brush the chicken breasts; season with pepper and salt.
2. Cook the chicken until completely done and no longer pink inside, six to seven minutes on each side. Take off from the heat, let rest for five minutes, then thinly slice.
3. Combine in a big mixing basin the mixed greens, shredded carrots, red cabbage, edamame, red bell pepper, green onions, and cilantro.
4. To make the dressing, whisk together in a small bowl the soy sauce, rice vinegar, sesame oil, honey, ginger, garlic, and sriracha (if using).
5. Incorporate the sliced grilled chicken into the salad mix. Drizzle the salad's dressing over it then gently toss to mix.
6. Just before dining, sprinkle with sliced almonds and sesame seeds.

Nutritional Information:

Chicken And Avocado Salad

4 SERVINGS **15 MINUTES** **10 MINUTES**

Ingredients:

- 2 cups cooked, shredded chicken breast
- 2 ripe avocados, diced
- 1 cup cherry tomatoes, halved
- 1/4 cup red onion, finely chopped
- 1/4 cup fresh cilantro, chopped
- 1/4 cup olive oil
- 2 tablespoons lime juice
- 1 teaspoon salt
- 1/2 teaspoon black pepper

Directions:

1. Combine the shredded chicken, sliced avocados, halved cherry tomatoes, and finely cut red onion in a big mixing basin.
2. Whisk together in a small bowl the olive oil, salt, lime juice, and black pepper until thoroughly blended.
3. Spoon the dressing over the chicken and veggie combo.
4. Till the dressing coats all the ingredients equally, gently toss everything together.
5. Over the salad, sprinkle the chopped fresh cilantro; then, gently mix one more.
6. For a chilled salad, serve straight away or refrigerated for up to two hours ahead.

Nutritional Information:

Calories: 320, Protein: 24g, Carbohydrates: 12g, Fat: 22g, Fiber: 6g, Cholesterol: 50 mg, Sodium: 600 mg, Potassium: 850 mg

Grilled Chicken And Quinoa Salad

4 SERVINGS 15 MINUTES 20 MINUTES

Ingredients:

- 2 medium boneless, skinless chicken breasts
- 1 cup quinoa
- 2 cups water
- 1 cup cherry tomatoes, halved
- 1 cucumber, diced
- 1 red bell pepper, diced
- 1/4 cup red onion, finely chopped
- 1/4 cup feta cheese, crumbled
- 2 tablespoons olive oil
- 2 tablespoons lemon juice
- 1 teaspoon dried oregano
- Salt and black pepper to taste
- Fresh parsley for garnish (optional)

Directions:

1. Preheat the grill to medium-high heat.
2. On both sides, seasons the chicken breasts with black pepper and salt.
3. Chicken breasts should be fully cooked after about six to seven minutes on each side under grill. Take them from the grill and let them cool for five minutes before cutting.
4. Rinse the quinoa with cool water in meantime. Bring the quinoa and water to a boil in a medium-pot. Cook for roughly 15 minutes or until the quinoa is soft and water has absorbed, lowering to a simmer under cover. Fluff using a fork; let it cool somewhat.
5. Combine the red bell pepper, red onion, cherry tomatoes, cucumber, and cooked quinoa in a big bowl.
6. Whisk together in a small bowl olive oil, lemon juice, salt, dried oregano, and black pepper.
7. Drizzle the quinoa mixture with the dressing then stir-through.
8. Cut the grilled chicken breasts then lay them on top of the salad.
9. If wanted, sprinkle feta cheese and top with fresh parsley.
10. For best tastes, serve straight away or refrigerate for half an hour.

Nutritional Information:

Calories: 350, Protein: 30g, Carbohydrates: 28g, Fat: 12g, Fiber: 5g, Cholesterol: 60mg, Sodium: 300mg, Potassium: 600mg

Chicken And Mango Salad

4 SERVINGS 20 MINUTES 15 MINUTES

Ingredients:

- 2 cups cooked chicken breast, diced or shredded
- 1 large mango, peeled and diced
- 4 cups mixed greens (spinach, arugula, and lettuce)
- 1 cup cherry tomatoes, halved
- 1/2 red onion, thinly sliced
- 1/4 cup fresh cilantro, chopped
- 1/4 cup sliced almonds, toasted
- 1/4 cup crumbled feta cheese
- 1 avocado, sliced
- 1 lime, juiced
- 2 tablespoons olive oil
- 1 tablespoon honey
- Salt and pepper, to taste

Directions:

1. Combine in a big mixing bowl the cooked chicken, chopped mango, mixed greens, cherry tomatoes, red onion, cilantro, sliced almonds, and crumbled feta cheese.
2. Whisk together in a small bowl the olive oil, lime juice, honey, salt, and pepper until thoroughly blended to make the dressing.
3. Drizzle the dressing over the salad mixture, then gently toss to evenly coat.
4. Set the avocado slices atop the salad.
5. Refrigerate for up to two hours before serving or straight away.

Nutritional Information:

Calories: 332, Protein: 26g, Carbohydrates: 22g, Fat: 18g, Fiber: 6g, Cholesterol: 72mg, Sodium: 210mg, Potassium: 810mg

Chicken And Bacon Ranch Salad

4 SERVINGS **15 MINUTES**

Ingredients:

- 2 cups diced grilled chicken breast
- 8 slices cooked bacon, chopped
- 4 cups chopped romaine lettuce
- 1 cup cherry tomatoes, halved
- 1/2 cup shredded cheddar cheese
- 1/4 cup red onion, thinly sliced
- 1/2 cup ranch dressing
- 1 avocado, sliced
- Salt and pepper to taste

Directions:

1. Combine chopped bacon and diced grilled chicken breast in a big mixing basin.
2. To the bowl include the chopped romaine lettuce, cherry tomatoes, shredded cheddar cheese, and red onion.
3. Spoon the ranch dressing over the salad assembly.
4. Till the dressing coats everything equally, gently toss all the ingredients together.
5. Set avocado slices atop the salad.
6. Taste should guide the season with salt and pepper.
7. Present quickly and savor!

Nutritional Information:

Calories: 420, Protein: 32g, Carbohydrates: 12g, Fat: 28g, Fiber: 6g, Cholesterol: 90mg, Sodium: 780mg, Potassium: 820mg

Chicken And Spinach Salad

4 SERVINGS **15 MINUTES** **10 MINUTES**

Ingredients:

- 2 cups cooked chicken breast, diced
- 6 cups fresh spinach leaves
- 1 cup cherry tomatoes, halved
- 1/2 cup red onion, thinly sliced
- 1/4 cup feta cheese, crumbled
- 1/4 cup sliced almonds, toasted
- 2 tbsp olive oil
- 1 tbsp balsamic vinegar
- 1 tsp Dijon mustard
- Salt and pepper, to taste

Directions:

1. Combine in a big bowl the cooked chicken, spinach leaves, cherry tomatoes, red onion, and feta cheese.
2. To make the dressing, whisk together in a small bowl the olive oil, balsamic vinegar, Dijon mustard, salt, and pepper.
3. Drizzle the salad components with the dressing; then, gently toss to mix.
4. On top before serving, sprinkle the roasted almonds.
5. Present right away and savor your aromatic Chicken and Spinach Salad.

Nutritional Information:

Calories: 310, Protein: 26g, Carbohydrates: 8g, Fat: 18g, Fiber: 3g, Cholesterol: 70 mg, Sodium: 420 mg, Potassium: 780 mg

Mediterranean Chicken Salad

🍽️ 4 SERVINGS ⏱️ 20 MINUTES 🕐 15 MINUTES

Ingredients:

- 2 cups cooked, shredded chicken breast
- 1 cup cherry tomatoes, halved
- 1/2 cup cucumber, diced
- 1/4 cup red onion, thinly sliced
- 1/4 cup Kalamata olives, pitted and chopped
- 1/4 cup feta cheese, crumbled
- 2 tablespoons fresh parsley, chopped
- 2 tablespoons fresh mint, chopped
- 3 tablespoons extra-virgin olive oil
- 2 tablespoons fresh lemon juice
- 1 teaspoon dried oregano
- 1/2 teaspoon salt
- 1/4 teaspoon black pepper
- Mixed salad greens, for serving

Directions:

1. Combine in a big bowl the shredded chicken, cherry tomatoes, cucumber, red onion, Kalamata olives, feta cheese, parsley, and mint.
2. Whisk in a small bowl the extra-virgin olive oil, fresh lemon juice, dried oregano, salt, and black pepper until well blended.
3. Drizzle the dressing over the salad mixture then gently toss to evenly coat every component.
4. Present mixed salad greens on a tray or on individual dishes.
5. Spoon the Mediterranean chicken salad across the greens.
6. Present right away and have fun!

Nutritional Information:

Calories: 320, Protein: 28g, Carbohydrates: 10g, Fat: 20g, Fiber: 3g, Cholesterol: 70mg, Sodium: 720mg, Potassium: 510mg

Chicken And Apple Salad

🍽️ 4 SERVINGS ⏱️ 15 MINUTES 🕐 10 MINUTES

Ingredients:

- 2 cups shredded cooked chicken breast
- 2 large apples, cored and diced
- 1/2 cup celery, thinly sliced
- 1/4 cup red onion, finely chopped
- 1/2 cup walnuts, chopped and toasted
- 1/3 cup dried cranberries
- 1/2 cup Greek yogurt
- 1/4 cup mayonnaise
- 2 tbsp lemon juice
- Salt and pepper to taste
- 4 cups mixed greens

Directions:

1. Combine in a large bowl shredded cooked chicken breast, diced apples, thinly sliced celery, finely chopped red onion, chopped and toasted walnuts, and dried cranberries.
2. Whisk Greek yogurt, mayonnaise, lemon juice, salt, and pepper until completely blended in a small basin.
3. Drizzle the dressing over the chicken mixture and toss until every bit is covered.
4. Top a bed of mixed greens with the chicken and apple mixture.
5. Straight away refrigerate any leftovers.

Nutritional Information:

Calories: 350, Protein: 25g, Carbohydrates: 28g, Fat: 17g, Fiber: 4g, Cholesterol: 55 mg, Sodium: 320 mg, Potassium: 550 mg

Chicken And Pineapple Salad

🍽️ 4 SERVINGS   ⏱️ 10 MINUTES   🕐 15 MINUTES

Ingredients:

- 2 cups cooked and diced chicken breast
- 1 cup fresh pineapple chunks
- 1/2 cup red bell pepper, diced
- 1/4 cup red onion, finely chopped
- 1/4 cup cilantro, chopped
- 1/4 cup sliced almonds
- 2 cups mixed salad greens
- 1/4 cup lime juice
- 2 tablespoons olive oil
- 1 tablespoon honey
- Salt and pepper to taste

Directions:

1. Combine in a large bowl shredded cooked chicken breast, diced apples, thinly sliced celery, finely chopped red onion, chopped and toasted walnuts, and dried cranberries.
2. Whisk Greek yogurt, mayonnaise, lemon juice, salt, and pepper until completely blended in a small basin.
3. Drizzle the dressing over the chicken mixture and toss until every bit is covered.
4. Top a bed of mixed greens with the chicken and apple mixture.
5. Straight away refrigerate any leftovers.

Nutritional Information:

Calories: 320, Protein: 30g, Carbohydrates: 20g, Fat: 14g, Fiber: 3g, Cholesterol: 70mg, Sodium: 150mg, Potassium: 620mg

---

Chicken And Chickpea Salad

🍽️ 4 SERVINGS   ⏱️ 15 MINUTES   🕐 10 MINUTES

Ingredients:

- 2 cups cooked chicken breast, diced
- 1 can (15 oz) chickpeas, rinsed and drained
- 1 cup cherry tomatoes, halved
- 1/2 red onion, finely chopped
- 1 cucumber, diced
- 1/4 cup fresh parsley, chopped
- 3 tbsp extra-virgin olive oil
- 2 tbsp lemon juice
- 1 tsp ground cumin
- Salt and pepper to taste

Directions:

1. Combine in a big mixing basin the chopped chicken, chickpeas, cherry tomatoes, red onion, cucumber, and fresh parsley.
2. Whisk ground cumin, salt, pepper, lemon juice, extra-virgin olive oil, in a small bowl.
3. Spoon the dressing over the chicken and chickpea mixture.
4. Toss carefully to guarantee the dressing coats all components equally.
5. Present straight away or chill for half an hour to let tastes marry. Refrigerate.

Nutritional Information:

Calories: 320, Protein: 28g, Carbohydrates: 23g, Fat: 15g, Fiber: 6g, Cholesterol: 50 mg, Sodium: 340 mg, Potassium: 690 mg

Buffalo Chicken Salad

4 SERVINGS 15 MINUTES 15 MINUTES

Ingredients:

- 2 cups cooked chicken breast, shredded
- 1/2 cup buffalo sauce
- 6 cups mixed greens (lettuce, arugula, spinach)
- 1 cup cherry tomatoes, halved
- 1/2 cup celery, diced
- 1/4 cup red onion, thinly sliced
- 1/2 cup blue cheese crumbles
- 1/4 cup ranch or blue cheese dressing
- 1 avocado, diced
- Salt and pepper to taste

Directions:

1. In a medium bowl, combine shredded chicken and buffalo sauce. Mix well until chicken is evenly coated.
2. Arange the mixed greens equally in a big salad bowl.
3. Top the greens with buffalo chicken, cherry tomatoes, celery, red onion, and avocado.
4. Sprinkle the blue cheese crumbles on top of the salad.
5. Drizzle the ranch or blue cheese dressing over the salad.
6. Toss the salad gently to combine all ingredients. Season with salt and pepper to taste.
7. Serve immediately.

Nutritional Information:

Calories: 320, Protein: 25g, Carbohydrates: 15g, Fat: 18g, Fiber: 5g, Cholesterol: 60mg, Sodium: 860mg, Potassium: 780mg

Chicken And Orzo Salad

4 SERVINGS 15 MINUTES 20 MINUTES

Ingredients:

- 1 cup orzo pasta
- 2 cups cooked and shredded chicken breast
- 1 cup cherry tomatoes, halved
- 1/2 cup red onion, finely chopped
- 1/2 cup Kalamata olives, pitted and sliced
- 1/4 cup fresh parsley, chopped
- 1/4 cup fresh basil, chopped
- 1/4 cup crumbled feta cheese
- 1/4 cup extra virgin olive oil
- 2 tablespoons red wine vinegar
- 1 tablespoon lemon juice
- 1 teaspoon dried oregano
- Salt and pepper to taste

Directions:

1. Use package directions to cook the orzo pasta. Drain and reserve to cool.
2. Combine in a big bowl cooked orzo, shredded chicken, cherry tomatoes, red onion, Kalamata olives, parsley, basil, and feta cheese.
3. Whisk in a small bowl olive oil, red wine vinegar, lemon juice, dried oregano, salt, and pepper.
4. Drizzle the dressing over the salad components and stir-through.
5. Before serving, let the salad sit for at least ten minutes so the flavors mingle.

Nutritional Information:

Calories: 370, Protein: 25g, Carbohydrates: 30g, Fat: 16g, Fiber: 3g, Cholesterol: 55mg, Sodium: 480mg, Potassium: 350mg

Chicken And Kale Salad

4 SERVINGS   **15 MINUTES**   **20 MINUTES**

Ingredients:

- 2 cups cooked, diced chicken breast
- 6 cups kale, chopped
- 1 cup cherry tomatoes, halved
- 1/2 cup red onion, thinly sliced
- 1/4 cup feta cheese, crumbled
- 1/4 cup sunflower seeds
- 1 lemon, juiced
- 3 tablespoons olive oil
- 1 tablespoon Dijon mustard
- 1 clove garlic, minced
- Pepper and Salt to taste

Directions:

1. To make the dressing, whisk together in a little bowl the lemon juice, olive oil, Dijon mustard, minced garlic, salt, and pepper.
2. Combine the half of the dressing and chopped kale in a big mixing basin. Spend two to three minutes massaging the kale with your hands until it begins to soften.
3. Add to the bowl with the greens the chopped chicken, cherry tomatoes, red onion, crumbled feta cheese, and sunflower seeds.
4. Drizzle the salad with the remaining dressing then toss to fully mix all the components.
5. For the flavors to merge, serve straight away or chill for up to one day.

Nutritional Information:

Calories: 320, Protein: 28g, Carbohydrates: 12g, Fat: 18g, Fiber: 4g, Cholesterol: 70 mg, Sodium: 450 mg, Potassium: 950 mg

Honey Mustard Chicken Salad

4 SERVINGS   **15 MINUTES**   **15 MINUTES**

Ingredients:

- 2 large boneless, skinless chicken breasts
- 4 cups mixed greens (lettuce, spinach, arugula)
- 1 cup cherry tomatoes, halved
- 1 large cucumber, sliced
- 1 medium red onion, thinly sliced
- 1 avocado, sliced
- 1/2 cup honey mustard dressing (store-bought or homemade)
- Salt and pepper to taste
- 1 tbsp olive oil

Directions:

1. Turn your grill or a grill pan over medium-high heat.
2. Olive oil brushes the chicken breasts; liberally sprinkle salt and pepper on both sides.
3. On each side, grill the chicken breasts for six to seven minutes, or until well done and no longer pink inside. Turn off the heat; let rest for a few minutes before slicing.
4. Prepare the salad components while the chicken grills. Combine in a big bowl the mixed greens, cherry tomatoes, cucumbers, red onion, and avocado.
5. Arange the thin slices of rested chicken breasts atop the salad.
6. Drizzle the salad with the honey mustard dressing then gently toss to mix.
7. Present right away so that every plate features some chicken and a nice combination of vegetables.

Nutritional Information:

Calories: 350, Protein: 30g, Carbohydrates: 20g, Fat: 20g, Fiber: 5g, Cholesterol: 75mg, Sodium: 600mg, Potassium: 980mg

Savory Meat Salads

Classic Beef Salad

🍽️ 4 SERVINGS ⏱️ 15 MINUTES 🕐 20 MINUTES

Ingredients:

- 1 lb Beef sirloin or ribeye, thinly sliced
- 2 tbsp Olive oil
- 1 tsp Salt
- 1/2 tsp Black pepper
- 1/4 cup Red onion, thinly sliced
- 1/2 cup Cherry tomatoes, halved
- 1/2 cup Cucumber, sliced
- 1/4 cup Fresh parsley, chopped
- 1/4 cup Feta cheese, crumbled
- 2 tbsp Balsamic vinegar
- 1 tbsp Dijon mustard
- 1 tbsp Honey
- 2 cups Mixed greens

Directions:

1. Put olive oil in a big pan and heat it over medium-high heat. Add salt and black pepper to the beef.
2. Put the meat slices in the pan and cook them for four to five minutes on each side, or until they are browned and done the way you like them. Take them out of the pan and give them a minute to rest.
3. Mix honey, Dijon mustard, and balsamic vinegar in a small bowl with a whisk to make the dressing.
4. Red onion, cherry tomatoes, cucumber, and fresh parsley should all be put in a big salad bowl.
5. Cut the beef into thin slices across the grain and put them in the salad bowl.
6. Pour the dressing over the salad and toss it gently to mix.
7. Add crumbled feta cheese on top.
8. Serve right away and enjoy!

Nutritional Information:

Calories: 320, Protein: 28g, Carbohydrates: 10g, Fat: 18g, Fiber: 3g, Cholesterol: 60mg, Sodium: 450mg, Potassium: 600mg

Steak And Blue Cheese Salad

🍽️ 4 SERVINGS ⏱️ 20 MINUTES 🕐 15 MINUTES

Ingredients:

- 1 lb sirloin steak
- 1 tbsp olive oil
- 1 tsp salt
- 1/2 tsp black pepper
- 6 cups mixed greens (such as arugula, spinach, and romaine)
- 1 cup cherry tomatoes, halved
- 1/2 red onion, thinly sliced
- 1/2 cup crumbled blue cheese
- 1/4 cup walnuts, toasted
- 1/4 cup balsamic vinaigrette

Directions:

1. Warm up the grill over medium-high heat.
2. Add salt and black pepper to the sirloin cut after rubbing it with olive oil.
3. Grill the steak for four to five minutes on each side, or until it's done the way you like it.
4. After taking the steak off the grill, let it rest for 5 minutes. Then, cut it into thin slices across the grain.
5. Put the mixed leaves, cherry tomatoes, and red onion in a large salad bowl.
6. Cracked blue cheese, toasted walnuts, and thin slices of steak should be put on top of the salad.
7. Add the balsamic dressing and gently toss everything together.
8. Serve right away.

Nutritional Information:

Calories: 360, Protein: 28g, Carbohydrates: 10g, Fat: 23g, Fiber: 3g, Cholesterol: 75mg, Sodium: 500mg, Potassium: 550mg

Pork And Apple Salad

4 SERVINGS   **15 MINUTES**   **10 MINUTES**

Ingredients:

- 300g pork tenderloin
- 2 medium apples, thinly sliced
- 1 small red onion, finely sliced
- 4 cups mixed salad greens
- 1/4 cup walnuts, toasted
- 2 tbsp olive oil
- 1 tbsp apple cider vinegar
- 1 tsp Dijon mustard
- Salt and pepper to taste

Directions:

1. Put your pan or grill on medium-high heat to warm it up. Season the pork chops with salt and pepper.
2. For about 5 minutes on each side, or until it's done, grill or sear it. Leave it alone for a while after taking it off the heat. After that, cut it into very thin pieces.
3. In a large salad bowl, mix together salad greens, apple slices, and red onion pieces.
4. Gather the olive oil, apple cider vinegar, and Dijon mustard in a small bowl. Use a whisk to mix them together. If you think it needs it, add more salt and pepper.
5. Toast the walnuts and then add them to the salad bowl with the pork that has been chopped.
6. Add the dressing to the salad and gently toss it to mix everything.
7. Enjoy your fresh Pork and Apple Salad right away.

Nutritional Information:

Calories: 320, Protein: 20g, Carbohydrates: 15g, Fat: 20g, Fiber: 3g, Cholesterol: 60mg, Sodium: 200mg, Potassium: 600mg

Lamb And Mint Salad

4 SERVINGS   **15 MINUTES**   **10 MINUTES**

Ingredients:

- 400 grams lamb, thinly sliced
- 2 tablespoons olive oil
- 1 teaspoon salt
- 1/2 teaspoon black pepper
- 1 teaspoon smoked paprika
- 100 grams mixed salad greens (rocket, spinach, watercress, etc.)
- 1/4 cup fresh mint leaves, chopped
- 1/2 red onion, thinly sliced
- 100 grams cherry tomatoes, halved
- 1 cucumber, sliced
- 1/4 cup crumbled feta cheese
- 2 tablespoons lemon juice
- 1 tablespoon balsamic vinegar
- 1 teaspoon Dijon mustard
- 1 garlic clove, minced

Directions:

1. Put the lamb pieces, olive oil, pepper, salt, and smoked paprika in a bowl.
2. As soon as the pan is hot, add the lamb slices and cook them for three to four minutes on each side, or until they are fully cooked.
3. Put the red onion, mint leaves, cherry tomatoes, mint leaves, cucumber, feta cheese, and salad greens in a big bowl.
4. To make the sauce, garlic, mix the basil, lemon juice, and Dijon mustard in a smaller bowl using a whisk.
5. Mix the cooked lamb slices into the salad.
6. Add the sauce to the salad and mix it all together.
7. Serve right away.

Nutritional Information:

Calories: 350, Protein: 25g, Carbohydrates: 10g, Fat: 22g, Fiber: 3g, Cholesterol: 60mg, Sodium: 580mg, Potassium: 500mg

Roast Beef And Arugula Salad

4 SERVINGS   **15 MINUTES**   **0 MINUTES**

Ingredients:

- 12 oz thinly sliced roast beef
- 4 cups fresh arugula
- 1 cup cherry tomatoes, halved
- 1/2 cup thinly sliced red onion
- 1/2 cup crumbled blue cheese
- 1/4 cup toasted pine nuts
- 1/4 cup balsamic vinaigrette

Directions:

1. Spread the fresh arugula evenly on a large serving platter.
2. Arrange the thinly sliced roast beef on top of the bed of arugula.
3. Scatter the cherry tomatoes, thinly sliced red onion, crumbled blue cheese, and toasted pine nuts evenly over the roast beef and arugula.
4. Drizzle the balsamic vinaigrette over the salad just before serving.
5. Toss lightly to combine all the ingredients, ensuring the dressing is evenly distributed.

Nutritional Information:

Calories: 310, Protein: 25g, Carbohydrates: 12g, Fat: 20g, Fiber: 2g, Cholesterol: 65mg, Sodium: 520mg, Potassium: 450mg

Ham And Cheddar Salad

4 SERVINGS   **15 MINUTES**   **0 MINUTES**

Ingredients:

- 2 cups chopped ham
- 1 cup shredded cheddar cheese
- 1 cup cherry tomatoes, halved
- 1/2 cup chopped red onion
- 1/4 cup chopped green bell pepper
- 1/4 cup sliced black olives
- 2 cups mixed salad greens
- 1/4 cup ranch dressing
- Cracked black pepper, to taste

Directions:

1. Cherry tomatoes, red onion, green bell pepper, black olives, and chopped ham should all be put in a big salad bowl.
2. Put the mixed salad greens in the bowl and gently toss to mix the items together.
3. Spread the ranch sauce on top of the salad.
4. Toss the salad one more time to make sure the dressing covers everything.
5. Add cracked black pepper to taste.
6. Serve right away or put in the fridge until you're ready to serve.

Nutritional Information:

Calories: 260, Protein: 17g, Carbohydrates: 9g, Fat: 17g, Fiber: 2g, Cholesterol: 50mg, Sodium: 800mg, Potassium: 350mg

Turkey And Cranberry Salad

🍽️ 4 SERVINGS   ⏱️ 15 MINUTES   🕐 0 MINUTES

Ingredients:

- 2 cups cooked turkey breast, diced
- 1 cup fresh cranberries, halved
- 2 cups mixed salad greens
- 1/2 cup chopped celery
- 1/4 cup chopped red onion
- 1/4 cup crumbled feta cheese
- 1/4 cup chopped walnuts
- 1/2 cup vinaigrette dressing (or your preferred salad dressing)

Directions:

1. Cut up the turkey and put it in a big salad bowl. Add the fresh cranberries, mixed salad greens, celery, and red onion.
2. Break up the feta cheese and chop the walnuts and add them to the bowl.
3. Put the vinaigrette sauce on top of the salad.
4. Gently toss everything together until everything is well mixed and the sauce covers everything evenly.
5. If you'd rather have a cold salad, put the salad in the fridge for 15 minutes and then serve.

Nutritional Information:

Calories: 320, Protein: 20g, Carbohydrates: 18g, Fat: 22g, Fiber: 4g, Cholesterol: 50mg, Sodium: 420mg, Potassium: 550mg

Bacon And Egg Salad

🍽️ 4 SERVINGS   ⏱️ 10 MINUTES   🕐 15 MINUTES

Ingredients:

- 8 slices bacon
- 4 large eggs
- 6 cups mixed greens (such as baby spinach, arugula, and romaine)
- 1 cup cherry tomatoes, halved
- 1 avocado, diced
- 1/4 cup red onion, thinly sliced
- 1/4 cup crumbled feta cheese
- 2 tablespoons olive oil
- 1 tablespoon balsamic vinegar
- Salt and pepper to taste

Directions:

1. Put the bacon in a big skillet and heat it over medium range. It will take about 8 to 10 minutes of cooking after adding the bacon slices until they are crispy. After letting the bacon drain on a paper towel-lined plate, break it up into small pieces that are easy to eat.
2. Boil the Eggs: Heat up a medium-sized pot of water while the bacon cooks. Carefully put the eggs into the boiling water, and cook them for 9 minutes to get firm whites. Put the eggs in a bowl of ice water for five minutes to cool down. Then peel and cut them into pieces.
3. Get the salad base ready: Mixed greens, cherry tomatoes, avocado, red onion, and feta cheese should all be put in a big salad bowl.
4. Get the dressing ready: Salt and pepper to taste should be mixed with the olive oil in a small bowl.
5. Put the salad together by putting the egg quarters and chopped bacon in a salad bowl. Pour the dressing over the salad and gently toss to mix.
6. Set the table: Put the salad on four plates and serve right away.

Nutritional Information:

Calories: 350, Protein: 15g, Carbohydrates: 10g, Fat: 28g, Fiber: 4g, Cholesterol: 210mg, Sodium: 600mg, Potassium: 600mg

Prosciutto And Melon Salad

4 SERVINGS   **10 MINUTES**   **0 MINUTES**

Ingredients:

- 8 slices Prosciutto
- 1 medium Cantaloupe, peeled, seeded, and sliced
- 4 cups Arugula
- 1 medium Red Onion, thinly sliced
- 1/4 cup Olive Oil
- 2 tbsp Balsamic Vinegar
- 1 tbsp Honey
- 1 tsp Black Pepper
- 1/2 tsp Sea Salt
- 1/4 cup Shaved Parmesan Cheese
- Fresh Basil leaves, for garnish

Directions:

1. Arrange the arugula evenly on four salad plates.
2. Place the cantaloupe slices over the arugula on each plate.
3. Drape the prosciutto slices over the cantaloupe and arugula.
4. Distribute the thinly sliced red onion over the salads.
5. In a small bowl, whisk together the olive oil, balsamic vinegar, honey, black pepper, and sea salt until well combined to make the dressing.
6. Drizzle the dressing evenly over the salads on each plate.
7. Sprinkle shaved Parmesan cheese over the salads.
8. Garnish each salad with fresh basil leaves.

Nutritional Information:

Calories: 280, Protein: 10g, Carbohydrates: 18g, Fat: 20g, Fiber: 2g, Cholesterol: 20 mg, Sodium: 780 mg, Potassium: 500 mg

Chorizo And Potato Salad

4 SERVINGS   **15 MINUTES**   **25 MINUTES**

Ingredients:

- 8 oz Chorizo sausage, sliced
- 1 lb Baby potatoes, halved
- 1 cup Cherry tomatoes, halved
- 1/2 Red onion, thinly sliced
- 1/4 cup Fresh parsley, chopped
- 3 tbsp Olive oil
- 1 tbsp Red wine vinegar
- 1 tsp Dijon mustard
- Salt and pepper, to taste

Directions:

1. Get the oven to 400°F/200°C.
2. Cut the baby potatoes in half and put them on a baking sheet. Put 1 tablespoon of olive oil on top and add salt and pepper to taste. The food should be soft and golden brown after 20 minutes.
3. Set the pan on medium-low heat while the potatoes cook. After you add the chorizo pieces, cook them for 6 to 7 minutes, or until they get crispy and brown. Take it off the heat and leave it alone.
4. It's time to make the sauce. In a small bowl, mix the red wine vinegar, Dijon mustard, salt, and pepper with the rest of the olive oil.
5. In a large bowl, mix the cooked chorizo, red onion, cherry tomatoes, and chopped parsley.
6. Give the salad a light toss after adding the sauce. It's fine to serve it hot or cold.

Nutritional Information:

Calories: 356, Protein: 14g, Carbohydrates: 28g, Fat: 21g, Fiber: 4g, Cholesterol: 37mg, Sodium: 750mg, Potassium: 560mg

Duck And Orange Salad

4 SERVINGS   **15 MINUTES**   **30 MINUTES**

Ingredients:

- 2 duck breasts
- 2 oranges
- 4 cups mixed salad greens
- 1/4 cup sliced red onions
- 1/4 cup crumbled blue cheese
- 1/4 cup walnut halves, toasted
- 1/4 cup pomegranate seeds (optional)
- 2 tablespoons balsamic vinegar
- 3 tablespoons olive oil
- Salt and pepper to taste

Directions:

1. Preheat the oven to 200°C/400°F.
2. Score the duck breast skin and season with salt and pepper.
3. Sear duck breasts, skin side down, in a medium-high heat pan for 5-7 minutes until crispy.
4. Flip the duck, transfer to the oven, and cook for 10-15 minutes until internal temp reaches 135°F (57°C) for medium-rare.
5. Rest the duck for 5 minutes, peel and segment the oranges, catching the juice in a bowl.
6. Whisk together orange juice, balsamic vinegar, and olive oil for the sauce.
7. Slice the duck breasts thinly.
8. Arrange mixed greens on a platter, top with duck slices, orange segments, red onion, blue cheese, walnuts, and optional pomegranate seeds.
9. Drizzle with the sauce and season with additional salt and pepper if needed.

Nutritional Information:

Calories: 450, Protein: 22g, Carbohydrates: 15g, Fat: 35g, Fiber: 4g, Cholesterol: 120 mg, Sodium: 300 mg, Potassium: 590 mg

Venison And Beet Salad

4 SERVINGS   **20 MINUTES**   **30 MINUTES**

Ingredients:

- 400 grams venison loin steak
- 4 medium beets, roasted and peeled
- 2 cups arugula
- 1/2 cup crumbled goat cheese
- 1/4 cup pecans, toasted
- 1 tablespoon olive oil
- 1 tablespoon balsamic vinegar
- 1 teaspoon Dijon mustard
- 1 clove garlic, minced
- Salt and pepper to taste

Directions:

1. Warm the oven up to 200°C (392°F). Put beets in aluminum foil and roast them for 30 minutes, or until they are soft. After it's cool, peel it and cut it into squares.
2. Put some olive oil in a grill or pan and heat it over medium-high heat while the beets roast.
3. Add salt and pepper to the deer loin steak. For medium-rare, cook for about 4 to 5 minutes on each side, or until done to your liking. After 5 minutes, cut it into thin slices.
4. Mix the olive oil, balsamic vinegar, Dijon mustard, chopped garlic, salt, and pepper in a small bowl using a whisk. This will make the dressing.
5. Put roasted beets, arugula, goat cheese, and toasted pecans in a big bowl and mix them together.
6. Place deer slices in a salad bowl and drizzle with the dressing that you just made. Carefully toss to mix.
7. Serve right away.

Nutritional Information:

Calories: 350, Protein: 30g, Carbohydrates: 20g, Fat: 18g, Fiber: 5g, Cholesterol: 70 mg, Sodium: 250 mg, Potassium: 900 mg

Sausage And Lentil Salad

4 SERVINGS   **15 MINUTES**   **20 MINUTES**

Ingredients:

- 8 oz (225g) smoked sausage, sliced
- 1 cup (200g) dry lentils
- 1 medium red onion, finely chopped
- 1 carrot, diced
- 1 celery stalk, diced
- 2 cups (475ml) chicken broth
- 2 tbsp olive oil
- 2 tbsp red wine vinegar
- 1 tbsp Dijon mustard
- Salt and pepper to taste
- 2 tbsp fresh parsley, chopped

Directions:

1. Run cold water over the beans and drain them.
2. Put lentils, chicken broth, and a pinch of salt in a medium pot. Bring to a boil, then lower the heat and let it cook for 18-20 minutes, or until the lentils are soft. Remove any extra juice and let it cool down.
3. Put the smoked sausage slices in a pan over medium-low heat. Cook for 5 to 6 minutes, until both sides are browned. Take it off the heat and set it aside.
4. Put the cooked lentils, red onion, carrot, and celery in a big bowl.
5. Mix the olive oil, red wine vinegar, Dijon mustard, salt, and pepper in a small bowl with a whisk.
6. Add the sauce to the lentil mix and mix it all together.
7. Mix the sausage slices that have been cooked into the salad slowly.
8. Before serving, sprinkle with fresh parsley.

Nutritional Information:

Calories: 320, Protein: 18g, Carbohydrates: 28g, Fat: 15g, Fiber: 11g, Cholesterol: 30mg, Sodium: 810mg, Potassium: 600mg

Chicken Liver And Onion Salad

4 SERVINGS   **15 MINUTES**   **20 MINUTES**

Ingredients:

- 1 lb Chicken Livers, trimmed
- 2 Tablespoons Olive Oil
- 1 Medium Onion, thinly sliced
- 3 Cups Mixed Salad Greens
- 1 Tablespoon Balsamic Vinegar
- 1 Tablespoon Dijon Mustard
- 1 Teaspoon Honey
- Salt and Pepper to taste
- 2 Tablespoons Fresh Parsley, chopped

Directions:

1. Set the Olive Oil on Low: Place the olive oil in a large pan and set it on low.
2. Cook the Onions: Put the sliced onions in the pan and cook for 5 to 7 minutes, until they are soft and clear.
3. How to cook the chicken livers: Place the chicken livers in the pan and push the onions to the side. The livers should be cooked for five to six minutes on each side, or until the middle is no longer pink.
4. Get the dressing ready: Put the honey, salt, pepper, and balsamic vinegar in a small bowl and mix them together while the livers are cooking.
5. Put together the salad. When the livers are done, take them out of the pan and let them cool down a bit. Then, cut the livers into pieces that are easy to eat.
6. Mix Them Together: Put the mixed salad greens, cooked onions, and sliced chicken livers in a big salad bowl.
7. Dress the Salad: Pour the sauce over the salad ingredients and gently toss to cover everything.
8. To make the salad look nicer, sprinkle the chopped parsley on top.

Nutritional Information:

Calories: 180, Protein: 22g, Carbohydrates: 8g, Fat: 6g, Fiber: 2g, Cholesterol: 400mg, Sodium: 340mg, Potassium: 400mg

Corned Beef And Cabbage Salad

 4 SERVINGS   15 MINUTES   10 MINUTES

Ingredients:

- 2 cups cooked corned beef, thinly sliced or shredded
- 4 cups shredded green cabbage
- 1 cup shredded carrots
- 1/2 cup sliced red onion
- 1/4 cup chopped fresh parsley
- 1/2 cup creamy horseradish dressing
- 1 tablespoon whole grain mustard
- Salt and pepper to taste

Directions:

1. Shred the green cabbage, carrots, and red onion and put them all in a big salad bowl.
2. Thinly slice or cut the corn beef and add it to the pan. Then, chop the fresh parsley. Sprinkle to mix.
3. Put the creamy horseradish sauce and whole grain mustard in a small bowl and mix them together with a whisk. Add more salt and pepper if you think it needs it.
4. Add the dressing to the salad and toss it gently so that everything is covered.
5. For a stronger taste, chill in the fridge for up to an hour before serving or serve right away.

Nutritional Information:

Calories: 220, Protein: 15g, Carbohydrates: 10g, Fat: 14g, Fiber: 3g, Cholesterol: 45 mg, Sodium: 750 mg, Potassium: 350 mg

Meatball And Pasta Salad

 4 SERVINGS   15 MINUTES   20 MINUTES

Ingredients:

- 1 pound ground beef
- 1/2 cup breadcrumbs
- 1/4 cup grated Parmesan cheese
- 1 large egg
- 2 cloves garlic, minced
- 1 teaspoon salt
- 1/2 teaspoon black pepper
- 8 ounces pasta (fusilli or penne works well)
- 2 cups cherry tomatoes, halved
- 1/2 cup red onion, thinly sliced
- 1/2 cup black olives, sliced
- 2 cups arugula or baby spinach
- 1/4 cup olive oil
- 2 tablespoons balsamic vinegar
- 1 tablespoon Dijon mustard
- Salt and pepper to taste

Directions:

1. Put breadcrumbs, egg, garlic, salt, and pepper in a big bowl. Add the ground beef and mix it all together. Mix everything together well.
2. Form the mixture into meatballs that are about an inch across.
3. Over medium heat, cook the meatballs in a large pan, turning them over a few times, for about 10 to 12 minutes, or until they are browned and cooked all the way through.
4. While the meatballs are cooking, boil a big pot of salted water and follow the directions on the package for cooking pasta. To cool down, drain and rinse with cold water.
5. Put cooked pasta, cherry tomatoes, red onion, black olives, and arugula in a big bowl.
6. Put olive oil, balsamic vinegar, Dijon mustard, salt, and pepper in a small bowl and mix them together with a whisk. Add the sauce to the pasta and toss to coat.
7. Put the cooked meatballs on top of the salad and slowly mix them in.
8. Serve right away or put in the fridge until you're ready to serve.

Nutritional Information:

Calories: 550, Protein: 28g, Carbohydrates: 42g, Fat: 30g, Fiber: 4g, Cholesterol: 105 mg, Sodium: 820 mg, Potassium: 740 mg

Conclusion

As we come to the end of this journey through the **Ultimate Salad Cookbook**, we hope you've discovered the endless possibilities that salads have to offer. From simple, everyday greens to vibrant, hearty meals, salads are a versatile and delicious way to incorporate more fresh ingredients into your diet.

Salad-making is an art that combines flavors, textures, and colors in a way that not only pleases the palate but also nourishes the body. Whether you're preparing a quick lunch for yourself or an impressive dish for a gathering, the recipes and techniques you've learned here will serve you well.

Remember, the key to a great salad lies in the quality of your ingredients, the balance of flavors, and the care you put into its preparation. Don't hesitate to experiment with new combinations and make each salad your own. The tips and tools we've covered will guide you, but your creativity is what will truly make your salads stand out.

Thank you for choosing this book as your guide to mastering the art of salad-making. We hope it inspires you to explore new culinary horizons and enjoy the process of creating delicious, healthy meals. Here's to a lifetime of fresh, flavorful salads that bring joy to your table!

Happy salad-making!

Index

A

Arugula And Parmesan Salad 12

Asian Chicken Salad 57

Asian Slaw With Peanut Dressing 21

B

Baby Greens With Balsamic Vinaigrette 15

Bacon And Egg Salad 68

Barley And Roasted Vegetable Salad 30

Bbq Chicken Salad 56

Beet And Goat Cheese Salad 18

Bell Pepper And Corn Salad 23

Bibb Lettuce With Dijon Dressing 17

Black-Eyed Pea Salad 35

Broccoli And Cheddar Salad 22

Brown Rice And Avocado Salad 33

Buffalo Chicken Salad 62

Bulgur And Parsley Salad 31

Butter Lettuce With Herbs 14

C

Cabbage And Apple Slaw 25

Calamari And Tomato Salad 51

Carrot And Beet Salad 27

Carrot And Raisin Salad 20

Chicken And Apple Salad 60

Chicken And Avocado Salad 57

Chicken And Bacon Ranch Salad 59

Chicken And Chickpea Salad 61

Chicken And Kale Salad 63

Chicken And Mango Salad 58

Chicken And Orzo Salad 62

Chicken And Pineapple Salad 61

Chicken And Spinach Salad 59

Chicken Liver And Onion Salad 71

Chickpea And Cucumber Salad 31

Chorizo And Potato Salad 69

Classic Beef Salad 65

Classic Chicken Caesar Salad 56

Classic Cobb Salad 14

Classic Coleslaw 20

Classic Egg Salad 42

Classic Tuna Salad 47

Corned Beef And Cabbage Salad 72

Couscous And Tomato Salad 32

Crab And Corn Salad 48

Crunchy Radish Salad 23

Cucumber And Mint Salad 18

Cucumber And Tomato Salad 21

Curried Tofu Salad 38

D

Deviled Egg Salad 42

Duck And Orange Salad 70

E

Egg And Avocado Salad 44

Egg And Bacon Salad 43

Egg And Cucumber Salad 45

Egg And Potato Salad 43

Egg And Tomato Salad 44

Endive And Orange Salad 17

F

Fennel And Orange Salad 27

Freekeh And Kale Salad 34

G

Garden Salad With Ranch Dressing 13

Green Bean And Almond Salad 16

Grilled Chicken And Quinoa Salad 58

Grilled Shrimp Caesar Salad 54

Grilled Tofu And Vegetable Salad 39

H

Ham And Cheddar Salad 67

Honey Mustard Chicken Salad 63

J

Jicama And Citrus Salad 22

K

Kale And Apple Salad 13

L

Lamb And Mint Salad 66
Lentil And Feta Salad 32
Lobster And Asparagus Salad 50

M

Mackerel And Beet Salad 53
Marinated Mushroom Salad 25
Meatball And Pasta Salad 72
Mediterranean Chicken Salad 60
Mediterranean Egg Salad 45
Mediterranean Farro Salad 29
Mixed Greens With Lemon Vinaigrette 11

O

Octopus And Olive Salad 52
Orzo And Spinach Salad 33

P

Pork And Apple Salad 66
Prawn And Watermelon Salad 51
Prosciutto And Melon Salad 69

Q

Quinoa And Black Bean Salad 29

R

Rainbow Slaw With Lime Dressing 24
Roast Beef And Arugula Salad 67
Romaine And Radish Salad 15

S

Salmon And Dill Salad 48
Sardine And Potato Salad 52
Sausage And Lentil Salad 71

Scallop And Mango Salad 49
Seafood Pasta Salad 50
Shrimp And Avocado Salad 47
Simple Caesar Salad 11
Smoked Salmon And Cucumber Salad 49
Snap Pea And Radish Salad 26
Spelt And Roasted Pepper Salad 36
Spicy Crab Salad 54
Spicy Kimchi Slaw 26
Spicy Tofu And Noodle Salad 40
Spinach And Strawberry Salad 12
Steak And Blue Cheese Salad 65

T

Tabbouleh Salad 36
Three-Bean Salad 34
Tofu And Avocado Salad 40
Tofu And Edamame Salad 41
Tofu And Mango Salad 39
Tofu And Spinach Salad 41
Tofu Caesar Salad 38
Tuna Niçoise Salad 53
Turkey And Cranberry Salad 68

V

Venison And Beet Salad 70

W

Watercress And Avocado Salad 16
Wheatberry And Pomegranate Salad 35
Wild Rice And Cranberry Salad 30

Z

Zucchini Ribbon Salad 24

Printed in Great Britain
by Amazon